ERWIN CHEMERINSKY

THE SUPREME COURT IN TRANSITION

OCTOBER TERM 2020

AMERICAN BAR ASSOCIATION
Judicial Division

Cover design by Kelly Book/ABA Design.
Interior design by Betsy Kulak/ABA Design.

Printed in the United States of America.

25 24 23 22 21   5 4 3 2 1

For my grandchildren,
Andrew, Sarah, and Amy

Contents

Preface

For more than 30 years, I have had the enormous pleasure and good fortune of regularly speaking at federal and state judicial conferences, bar meetings, and other events to present a review of the Supreme Court's term. Bob Edmunds and Herbert Dixon kindly reached out to me and suggested putting the talk on the October 2020 Term into a short book, written soon after the Court handed down its decisions. The American Bar Association expressed interest in publishing this, and I was delighted to undertake it.

My goal, as in my talks, is to present the cases as clearly as I can and to explain their implications. My hope is to do this in a neutral manner, without evaluating them or editorializing. I certainly have views about many of them and cannot pretend that they do not sometimes affect my presentation of the cases. But my goal is to present the cases as fairly as I can and leave my normative judgments to be expressed in other places.

If there is interest, the goal would be to continue to do this each year at the end of the Supreme Court's term. I would welcome suggestions from readers on how to make this more useful.

I want to express my great appreciation to my research assistants—Haley Broughton, Summer Elliot, and Benji Martinez—for their terrific assistance. And as always, my wonderful assistant, Whitney Mello, was invaluable. Alex Chemerinsky provided excellent suggestions on many of the chapters and he and Catherine Fisk talked through many of the ideas in the book.

1

Introduction to October Term 2020

The most important development in the Supreme Court in the last year was the death of Justice Ruth Bader Ginsburg on September 18, 2020, and the confirmation of her successor, Justice Amy Coney Barrett on October 26, 2020. I neither want to overstate the significance of this nor underestimate its importance.

A statistic from the prior term—October Term 2019—is particularly revealing. That term the Court decided 53 cases with signed opinions after briefing and oral argument. Fourteen were decided by a 5–4 margin. In 10 of the 14, the majority was Chief Justice Roberts and Justices Thomas, Alito, Gorsuch, and Kavanaugh. Had Barrett been on the Court rather than Ginsburg, based on all we know of Barrett's judicial ideology, these cases likely would have been 6–3 rather than 5–4 decisions. In other words, her presence would not have changed the outcome in the cases, just the size of the majority.

But there were two 5–4 decisions where the majority was composed of Chief Justice Roberts and Justices Ginsburg, Breyer, Sotomayor, and Kagan. They involved important rulings striking down a Louisiana restriction on abortion[1] and invalidating President Trump's recission of the Deferred

Action for Childhood Arrival Program.[2] These cases likely would have come out differently with Barrett instead of Ginsburg on the Court.

Simple arithmetic shows that it will be much harder for the liberal justices to be in the majority in 5–4 decisions. They need to get two votes rather than one and they need to do so on a Court with five very conservative justices—Thomas, Alito, Gorsuch, Kavanaugh, and Barrett—and one more moderate conservative, Roberts.

The statistics from October Term 2020 confirm this prediction and the importance of this change in the membership of the Court. One would expect a large number of 6–3 decisions now, with six justices who were appointed by Republican Presidents and three justices who were appointed by Democratic Presidents. And that is exactly what happened. The Court decided 54 cases after briefing and oral argument. Twelve were decided 6–3 and another six were decided 5–4. There were no 5–4 decisions where the liberal justices were in the majority.

It is important to note the small number of cases decided by the Court. The term before, when the Court decided 53 cases, it was the smallest number in a year since 1862. This might have been attributed, in part, to the Court having cancelled oral arguments in March and April 2020 because of the COVID-19 pandemic and rescheduling some of them for May but putting off others until October. But this term without any arguments being postponed, the Court decided just 54 cases, the second smallest number since 1862, with only last year having fewer. As recently as the 1980s, the Court was deciding over 160 cases a term. In the last year of the Rehnquist Court, October Term 2004, it was down to 85 cases. But 53 and 54 decisions are stunningly few.

Everyone expected that the Roberts Court with three justices picked by President Donald Trump would be conservative and overall it was in October 2020. The justice least often in the majority was its most liberal member, Sonia Sotomayor, followed by the other two justices appointed by Democratic Presidents, Stephen Breyer and Elena Kagan. Interestingly, the justice most often in the majority—in 97% of the decisions—was Brett Kavanaugh.

It is hard to identify any case where the liberal position prevailed, except perhaps for the dismissal on standing grounds to the challenge to the Patient Protection and Affordable Care Act.[3] Also, it must be noted that the Supreme Court did not get involved in the 2020 election and perhaps staying out of the political fray was one of the most important things the Court did all year.

The conservative victories most notably included decisions concerning the Voting Rights Act[4] and the expansion of the protection of free exercise of religion.[5] There were less high profile, but important, conservative victories in cases restricting standing,[6] limiting presidential removal power,[7] expanding the protections of the Takings Clause,[8] and lessening the protections of juveniles accused of homicides.[9]

Some of the most important rulings cannot be easily described in ideological terms. In an 8–1 decision the Court strongly protected student speech over social media.[10] And there were crucial decisions concerning antitrust and copyright law.[11]

The most socially divisive legal issues—abortion, guns, affirmative action—were not before the Court. But the Court already has granted review in cases involving abortion and guns for October Term 2021 and a major affirmative action case may be added to the docket.

It is crucial to remember that the current conservative Court is likely to last a long time. At the time she was confirmed, Amy Coney Barrett was 48 years old. If she remains on the Court until she is 87—the age at which Justice Ginsburg died—Barrett will be a justice until the year 2059. At the time of her confirmation, Neil Gorsuch was 53, Brett Kavanaugh 55, John Roberts 65, Samuel Alito 70, and Clarence Thomas 72. It is easy to imagine these justices being together a decade or more.

It is always tempting to draw broad conclusions about what a Supreme Court term means. But it is crucial to remember not to generalize too much from a small sample. This is just one year in the Supreme Court, but an important one. I believe it should be regarded as a transitional year for the Court, as it lost a prominent liberal voice and gained a new conservative justice, and adapted to the reality of a third of its members having been added since 2017.

In the pages that follow, I look at the Supreme Court's decisions concerning antitrust and college sports, bankruptcy law, civil rights litigation, criminal law and procedure, federal court jurisdiction, First Amendment religion and speech, immigration law, Indian law, intellectual property, personal jurisdiction, separation of powers, the Takings Clause, and voting rights. Admittedly, I do not cover every decision of the term and have made choices as to which are most likely to be significant. My goal in each area is to clearly explain the decisions and to discuss their likely implications for lawyers, judges, and the law.

Endnotes

1. June Medical Services v. Russo, 140 S. Ct. 2103 (2020).
2. Department of Homeland Security v. Regents of University of California, 140 S. Ct. 1891 (2020).
3. California v. Texas, 141 S. Ct. 2104 (2021).
4. Bronvich v. Democratic National Committee, 141 S. Ct. 2321 (2021).
5. *See, e.g.*, Fulton v. City of Philadelphia, 141 S. Ct. 1868 (2021).
6. *See, e.g.*, TransUnion LLC v. Ramirez, 141 S. Ct. 2190 (2021).
7. Yellen v. Collins, 141 S. Ct. 1761 (2021).
8. Cedar Point Nursery v. Hassim, 141 S. Ct. 2063) (2021).
9. Jones v. Mississippi, 141 S. Ct. 1307 (2021).
10. Mahanoy Area School Dist. v. B.L., 141 S. Ct. 2038 (2021).
11. Google v. Oracle, 141 S. Ct. 1183 (2021); NCAA v. Alston, 141 S. Ct. 2141 (2021).

2

Antitrust and College Sports

One of the cases that received the most media attention this year was *National Collegiate Athletic Association v. Alston*.[1] Although the actual holding was limited in scope, the case itself portends major changes in how the NCAA can regulate college sports and impose limits on the benefits that collegiate athletes receive.

Facts

Shawne Alston earned an athletic scholarship to play football at West Virginia University in 2009. The money gave him the ability to work towards a degree, an opportunity hard to come by in the low-income Virginia neighborhood where he was raised. Despite the generous financial aid, "[h]e often went to bed hungry" because his scholarship didn't cover basic living necessities, like groceries.[2] A full-ride scholarship is only full by name for a majority of college football players. According to a study published by the National College Players Association in 2011 (the beginning of Alston's senior year), more than 80 percent of collegiate football players lived below the poverty line.[3] The issue Alston faced, along with countless other collegiate athletes, has become worse over time.[4] Under NCAA rules, Alston and other athletes can be given only tuition, room and board, and payment for books. Despite these statistics, the NCAA has for years insisted that their definition of amateur status of college athletes needed to be preserved through limits on compensation. Otherwise, they warned there would be no distinction between college athletics and professional athletics. This discrepancy between the players' needs and NCAA compensation has been at the forefront of several lawsuits.

NCAA v. Alston came about after the legal team which represented former UCLA basketball player Edward O'Bannon in a challenge to NCAA restrictions approached Alston about starting another lawsuit over the matter of living expenses and athletic scholarships. Alston agreed to become the lead plaintiff in a class action suit brought on behalf of Division I college basketball and football players. The case quickly became bigger than Alston imagined once it was consolidated with other cases. The federal district court focused on the restrictions on colleges and universities providing educational benefits to athletes, such as laptop computers, musical instruments, and graduate fellowships.

The district court found that NCAA's restrictions on these benefits violated federal antitrust law, but the court did not disturb the NCAA's rules limiting undergraduate athletic scholarships or other compensation related to athletic performance. The United States Court of Appeals for the Ninth Circuit affirmed the finding of antitrust liability and observed that "the NCAA and its member schools have the 'power to restrain student-athlete compensation in any way and at any time they wish, without any meaningful risk of diminishing their market dominance.'"[5]

Supreme Court Rules for Athletes

The Supreme Court unanimously affirmed that the NCAA restrictions on educational benefits violated federal antitrust law. The players did not appeal the issue concerning whether restrictions on compensation violated antitrust law, so that issue was not before the Court. Justice Neil Gorsuch wrote the opinion and agreed with Alston and other current and former players in their assertion that the NCAA violated § 1 of the Sherman Act by "agreeing to restrict the compensation colleges and universities may offer the student-athletes who play for their teams."[6] Section 1 of the Sherman Act prohibits "every contract, combination in the form of trust or otherwise, or conspiracy in restraint of trade or commerce."[7]

Justice Gorsuch traced the history of compensation of college athletes, pointing out that intercollegiate sports is big business:

> *At the center of this thicket of associations and rules sits a massive business. The NCAA's current broadcast contract for the March Madness basketball tournament is worth $1.1 billion annually. Its television deal for the FBS conference's College Football Playoff is worth approximately $470 million per year. Beyond these sums, the Division I conferences earn substantial revenue from regular-season games. For example, the Southeastern Conference (SEC) made more than $409 million in revenues from television contracts alone in 2017, with its total conference revenues exceeding $650 million that year. All these amounts have increased consistently over the years . . . The president of the NCAA earns nearly $4 million per year. Commissioners of the top conferences take home between $2 to $5 million. College athletic directors average more than $1 million annually. And annual salaries for top Division I college football coaches approach $11 million, with some of their assistants making more than $2.5 million.*[8]

The Court's choice to begin with this information reveals its view of big-time collegiate athletics. It evidences a recognition that there are enormous profits involved in college sports, yet relatively little of that money goes to the players.

The NCAA argued that "the district court went too far by weakening its restraints on education-related compensation and benefits."[9] But the Supreme Court emphasized the NCAA's monopoly control and its "admitted horizontal price fixing."[10] This makes it an atypical antitrust case. Normally, the court would be determining whether or not a party is enjoying complete control over a market. But here the NCAA did not contest its monopoly or that its restraints can harm what players can receive, as "student-athletes have nowhere else to sell their labor."[11] The Court explained:

> *[The NCAA does not] contest that [it] enjoys monopoly (or, as it's called on the buyer side, monopsony) control in that labor market—such that it is capable of depressing wages below competitive levels and restricting the quantity of student-athlete labor. Nor does the NCAA dispute that its member schools compete fiercely for student-athletes but remain subject to NCAA-issued-and-enforced limits on what compensation they can offer. Put simply, this suit involves admitted horizontal price fixing in a market where the defendants exercise monopoly control.*[12]

Instead, the NCAA argued that its monopoly control is necessary in order to facilitate fair competition amongst rivals and preserve amateurism in athletics. Justice Gorsuch quoted the brief of the NCAA:

> *The NCAA plays a critical role in the maintenance of a revered tradition of amateurism in college sports. There can be no question but that it needs ample latitude to play that role, or that the preservation of the student-athlete in higher education adds richness and diversity to intercollegiate athletics and is entirely consistent with the goals of the Sherman Act.*[13]

The Court was skeptical of the NCAA's stance, saying that the peculiar "intersection of higher education, sports, and money" at which the NCAA sits is not a compelling reason for the court to grant immunity from the Sherman Act.[14] Justice Gorsuch wrote that if the NCAA wants modifications in antitrust laws, it must request them from Congress. This is consistent with antitrust challenges to the National Football League and the National Basketball Association, where the Court held that if there was to be an antitrust exemption for them, it must come from Congress.[15] The antitrust exemption for baseball is regarded by the Court as a historical aberration, a rule not to be followed unless Congress changes the law to mandate accordingly.[16]

Justice Gorsuch agreed with the Ninth Circuit's application of the "rule of reason" test for assessing antitrust violations, which comes from *Ohio v. American Express Co.*[17] The three-part test under *American Express*'s framework requires the following elements: (1) that plaintiffs can prove that the challenged restraints produce significant anticompetitive effects in the relevant market; (2) whether the defendant can muster a procompetitive rationale for its restraints; (3) that plaintiffs can show that there are substantially less restrictive alternative rules that would achieve the same procompetitive effect as the challenged set of rules.[18] Analysis for step 2 cannot happen until step 1 is satisfied; analysis for step 3 cannot happen until step 2 is satisfied. The court noted how rare it was for antitrust inquiries to advance beyond step 1, as "courts have disposed of nearly all rule of reason cases in the last 45 years on the ground that the plaintiff failed to show a substantial anticompetitive effect."[19]

Justice Gorsuch's opinion acknowledged the NCAA's request that judges and justices should not make hardline rules for markets about which they have limited knowledge. The Court, however, concluded that the district court's factual findings adequately satisfied their final decree. Justice Gorsuch noted how "[u]nder the current decree, the NCAA is free to forbid in-kind benefits unrelated to a student's actual education; nothing stops it from enforcing a 'no Lamborghini' rule."[20]

Simply put, *NCAA v. Alston* is important because the Court emphatically rejects that the NCAA is immune from antitrust liability. More subtly, the case is significant because it reveals the Court's view of the NCAA. They see college sports as big business. They are clearly dubious about rules limiting college athletes' share of the huge dollars involved in collegiate sports, which student athletes help to generate.

Justice Kavanaugh wrote a concurring opinion that was even more forceful in expressing disapproval of the NCAA's restrictions on compensation for college athletes. His concurrence was called "the most anti-NCAA, damning antitrust opinion that has ever been authored" by Gabe Feldman, the director of the sports law program at Tulane University in New Orleans.[21] Justice Kavanaugh echoed how important it was that the Court found that the NCAA violated antitrust laws, as it had "long shielded its compensation rules from ordinary antitrust scrutiny."[22] He noted that this case involves just one of many restrictions imposed by the NCAA. He wrote:

> *But this case involves only a narrow subset of the NCAA's compensation rules—namely, the rules restricting the education-related benefits that student athletes may receive, such as post-eligibility scholarships at graduate or vocational schools. The rest of the NCAA's compensation rules are not at issue here and therefore remain on the books. Those remaining compensation rules generally restrict student athletes from receiving compensation or benefits from their colleges for playing sports. And those rules have also historically restricted student athletes from receiving money from endorsement deals and the like. I add this concurring opinion to underscore that the NCAA's remaining compensation rules also raise serious questions under the antitrust laws.*[23]

Justice Kavanaugh left no doubt on where he will come down if these restrictions are challenged in the future. He wrote:

> *The NCAA nonetheless asserts that its compensation rules are procompetitive because those rules help define the product of college sports. Specifically, the NCAA says that colleges may decline to pay student athletes because the defining feature of college sports, according to the NCAA, is that the student athletes are not paid. In my view, that argument is circular and unpersuasive. The NCAA couches its arguments for not paying student athletes in innocuous labels. But the labels cannot disguise the reality: The NCAA's business model would be flatly illegal in almost any other industry in America.*[24]

Justice Kavanaugh saw everyone in the industry profiting, except the athletes who play the actual sports:

> *The bottom line is that the NCAA and its member colleges are suppressing the pay of student athletes who collectively*

> *generate billions of dollars in revenues for colleges every year. Those enormous sums of money flow to seemingly everyone except the student athletes. College presidents, athletic directors, coaches, conference commissioners, and NCAA executives take in six- and seven-figure salaries. Colleges build lavish new facilities. But the student athletes who generate the revenues, many of whom are African American and from lower-income backgrounds, end up with little or nothing.*[25]

Lest anyone has doubts as to how Justice Kavanaugh will rule when there are challenges to the other restrictions on compensation imposed by the NCAA, he concluded his opinion by declaring: "The NCAA is not above the law."[26]

Implications

The *Alston* ruling itself is narrow and does little to rectify Shawne Alston's initial concerns. The Court's decision in *Alston* means the NCAA is now unable to prohibit colleges from providing things like laptops or musical instruments to student-athletes when the need is connected to their educational success, as long as the cost does not exceed approximately $6,000. It will take further litigation to determine whether the *Alston* holding extends to basic necessities like food, clothing, or rent. But that litigation, and other challenges to NCAA rules limiting compensation, are sure to come. The Court's unanimous ruling expresses great sympathy for college athletes and disdain for the NCAA. In sum, *NCAA v. Alston* may be limited in scope, but it foretells much broader changes over the NCAA's authority to impose restrictions on compensation for student athletes that are sure to come.

Endnotes

1. 141 S. Ct. 2141 (2021).
2. Ben Strauss, *Ex-Athlete's Battle for Scholarship Upgrades: 'I Feel Like I Helped My Brothers,'* N.Y. Times (Feb. 12, 2017), https://www.nytimes

.com/2017/02/12/sports/a-football-scholarship-is-a-full-ride-but-it-doesnt-mean-a-free-one.html?smid=url-share; *see also* Ben Strauss, *Athletes Stand to Gain in a Settlement with the* N.C.A.A, N.Y. Times (Feb. 4, 2017), https://www.nytimes.com/2017/02/04/sports/ncaa-player-antitrust-settlement-scholarships.html.

3. Ramogi Huma & Ellen J. Staurowsky, "The Price of Poverty in Big Time College Sport" 16 (2011), https://www.ncpanow.org/research/study-the-price-of-poverty-in-big-time-college-sport.

4. *See* Romogi Huma et al., "How the NCAA's Empire Robs Predominantly Black Athletes of Billions in Generational Wealth" (2020), https://www.ncpanow.org/studies-and-revenue/study-how-the-ncaas-empire-robs-predominantly-black-athletes-of-billions-in-generational-wealth.

5. *Alston*, 141 S. Ct. at 2152 (quoting another source).

6. *Id.* at 2147.

7. Sherman Act, 15 U.S.C § 1 (2004).

8. 141 S. Ct. at 2150–51 (quotations omitted) (citations omitted).

9. *Id.* at 2154.

10. *Id.*

11. *Id.* at 2156.

12. *Id.* at 2154.

13. *Id.* at 2157 (quoting Nat'l Collegiate Athletic Ass'n v. Bd. of Regents of the Univ. of Oklahoma, 468 U.S. 85, 120 (1984)).

14. *Id.* at 2159.

15. Peter A. Carfagna, Sports and the Law: Examining the Legal Evolution of America's Three "Major Leagues," 81–82 (3rd ed. 2017).

16. *See* Flood v. Kuhn, 407 U.S. 258 (1972) (upholding antitrust exemption for baseball).

17. Ohio v. Am. Express Co., 138 S. Ct. 2274 (2018).

18. *Alston*, 141 S. Ct. at 2161-62.

19. *Id.* at 2161.

20. *Id.* at 2165.

21. Adam Liptak & Alan Blinder, *Supreme Court Backs Payments to Student-Athletes in N.C.A.A. Case*, N.Y. Times (June 21, 2021), https://www.nytimes.com/2021/06/21/us/supreme-court-ncaa-student-athletes.html.

22. *Alston*, 141 S. Ct. at 2166 (Kavanaugh, J., concurring).

23. *Id.* at 2166–67 (Kavanaugh, J., concurring).

24. *Id.* at 2167.

25. *Id.* at 2168.

26. *Id.* at 2169.

3

Bankruptcy

The Court decided only one bankruptcy case in October 2020: *City of Chicago v. Fulton*.[1] The Bankruptcy Code provides that filing for bankruptcy creates an automatic stay of civil proceedings in other courts. This is to protect the debtor's interests by staying efforts to collect debts outside the bankruptcy forum. The issue in *City of Chicago v. Fulton* is whether an entity has an affirmative obligation to return passively retained property to a debtor or trustee immediately upon filing a bankruptcy petition under the Bankruptcy Code's automatic stay, provision 11 U.S.C § 362.

There are automatic consequences to filing a petition for bankruptcy. Under the Bankruptcy Code, filing for bankruptcy triggers the creation of an estate that holds all legal or equitable interests of the debtor in property as of the commencement of the case. Section 542 of the Code provides that an entity in possession of property of the bankruptcy case must deliver it to the trustee and account for that property.

Another consequence of filing for bankruptcy is that the petition creates a stay, applicable to all entities, of efforts to collect from the debtor outside of the bankruptcy forum. The stay prohibits any act to obtain possession of property of the estate or of property from the estate or *to exercise control over property of the estate*.

City of Chicago v. Fulton has straightforward facts. Several individuals whose cars had been impounded by the City filed for bankruptcy. Each of the vehicles had been impounded for the failure to pay fines for motor vehicle infractions. Each of these individuals subsequently filed for Chapter 13 bankruptcy and asked the City to return the vehicles. The City refused, and the lower courts held that the refusal violated the automatic stay provision of the Bankruptcy Code.

The Supreme Court reversed in a unanimous decision. Justice Alito wrote the opinion for the Court and Justice Sotomayor wrote a concurring opinion. The Court held the mere retention of estate property after the filing of a bankruptcy petition does not violate the automatic stay provision of 11 U.S.C. § 3762(a)(3). In other words, the City could continue to keep possession of the cars for those individuals who had filed bankruptcy.

Justice Alito focused on the language of the relevant provision of the Bankruptcy Code including words such as "stay," "act," and "exercise control." He said that these indicate that merely retaining possession of estate property doesn't violate the automatic stay. Only affirmative acts that would disturb the status quo of estate property that was held at the commencement of the bankruptcy petition are prohibited. Interestingly, as is increasingly common in the Roberts Court, Justice Alito relied on dictionary definitions of these words. He said that "stay" is commonly used to describe an order that suspends judicial alteration of the status quo, while "act" means something done or performed, and to "exercise" something like control means to put in practice or carry out in action.[2]

Put together, these three major elements of the provision mean that the section prohibits any affirmative act that would alter the status quo that existed at the time the bankruptcy petition is filed. Justice Alito noted that this does not mean that omissions can't qualify as acts in certain contexts, or that control can't mean to have power over something. But saying someone engages in an act to exercise control over a thing implies that something more than merely retaining control over property is required.

The Court stressed that "[a]ny ambiguity in the text of § 362(a)(3) is resolved decidedly in the City's favor by the existence of a separate provision, § 542, that expressly governs the turnover of estate property."[3] Section 542(a), with two exceptions, provides:

> *[A]n entity, other than a custodian, in possession, custody, or control, during the case, of property that the trustee may use,*

sell, or lease under section 363 of this title, or that the debtor may exempt under section 522 of this title, shall deliver to the trustee, and account for, such property or the value of such property, unless such property is of inconsequential value or benefit to the estate.

The Court explained that reading the automatic stay provision, § 362(a)(3), to cover mere retention of property would create two significant problems. First, it would render the central command of § 542 superfluous. Section 542 governs the requirement to turnover of property to the estate. Reading § 362 to include mere retention of property would make § 542 only surplusage. This, the Court says, is a reason why mere retention of property should not be enough to trigger the automatic stay provision.

In fact, the Court said that applying the automatic stay in this case would render commands of § 362(a)(3) and § 542 contradictory. Section 532 carves out exceptions to the turnover command, with (a) creating an exception for property of inconsequential value or benefit to the estate. Requiring the turnover of property in cases where § 542 exceptions apply, § 342 would require turnover of the property. The Court says that it would be an odd construction of § 362 to require a creditor to do immediately what § 542 specifically excludes.

Justice Alito said that the history of the Bankruptcy code confirms this textual interpretation.[4] Both § 362(a)(3) and § 542(a) were included in the original 1978 code. Originally, the stay applied only to any act to obtain possession of property of the estate. The phrase "or to exercise control over property of the estate" was not added until 1984. No one seriously disputes that the Code did not enforce a turnover obligation before 1984. To say that a turnover obligation was made in the 1984 amendment would mark an important change in the law. The Court says that it would have been odd for Congress to make this change by only adding the phrase "exercise control," without any cross-reference between the relevant provisions. The Court said that it is more accurate to say that the 1984 amendment added the phrase "exercise control" to simply extend the stay to acts that would change the status quo to tangible property without literally obtaining such property.

Justice Sotomayor wrote a concurring opinion.[5] She said that she joined the Court's opinion because she agrees that the Code does not cover a creditor's passive retention of property that was lawfully seized prebankruptcy. But she wrote separately to note that the Court has not decided whether and when § 362(a)'s other provisions may require a creditor to return a debtor's property. The Court also has not addressed how bankruptcy courts should enforce creditors' separate obligation to deliver estate property to the trustee or debtor under § 542(a).

Justice Sotomayor argued that the City's policy of refusing to return impounded vehicles runs counter with the spirit of the Bankruptcy Code, which is to give a fresh start to debtors. She wrote: "Regardless of whether the City's policy of refusing to return impounded vehicles satisfies the letter of the Code, it hardly comports with its spirit. The principal purpose of the Bankruptcy Code is to grant a 'fresh start' to debtors."[6]

Justice Sotomayor stressed the real-world impact of allowing the City to keep possession of the car. In Chapter 13 bankruptcy, a debtor works toward completing a court-approved repayment plan. It requires that debtors continue earning an income. To continue with employment, having a car is essential. This policy makes it hard for debtors to do so. Justice Sotomayor spoke of a vicious cycle that ensues:

> *Drivers in low-income communities across the country face similar vicious cycles: A driver is assessed a fine she cannot immediately pay; the balance balloons as late fees accrue; the local government seizes the driver's vehicle, adding impounding and storage fees to the growing debt; and the driver, now without reliable transportation to and from work, finds it all but impossible to repay her debt and recover her vehicle. Such drivers may turn to Chapter 13 bankruptcy for a fresh start. But without their vehicles, many debtors quickly find themselves unable to make their Chapter 13 payments. The cycle thus continues, disproportionately burdening communities of color, and interfering not only with debtors' ability to earn an income and pay their creditors but also with their access to childcare, groceries, medical appointments, and other necessities.*[7]

Justice Sotomayor noted that Court left open the possibility for relief under § 542(a), which requires an entity to turn over property belonging to the bankruptcy estate. But she also noted that this is a very slow process.

In the end, though obviously sympathetic to the debtors, Justice Sotomayor concluded that any gap left by the Court's ruling should be addressed by lawmakers and policymakers, not bankruptcy judges. The Advisory Committee on Rules of Bankruptcy Procedure should amend the Rules to ensure prompt resolution of debtors' requests for turnover. She also noted that Congress could act by amending the statute to guarantee expedited review or by enacting a new statutory mechanism that makes creditors return cars to debtors in a timely manner.

The Court's decision was very much based on its analysis of the statutory language and the structure of the Bankruptcy Code. But quite importantly, Justice Sotomayor explained how this will affect people's lives and stresses that there can be fixes through amendments to the Bankruptcy rules or by statutory changes.

Endnotes

1. Chicago v. Fulton, 141 U.S 585 (2021).
2. *Id.* at 590.
3. *Id.*
4. *Id.* at 591.
5. *Id.* at 592 (Sotomayor, J., concurring).
6. *Id.* at 593.
7. *Id.* at 593–94.

4

Civil Rights Litigation

Per curiam decisions handed down without briefing and oral argument generally do not get much attention, so it is understandable that the Court's ruling about qualified immunity in *Taylor v. Riojas* may have been completely overlooked—even by civil rights lawyers.[1] Yet *Taylor* is very significant. It is a rare instance in which the Supreme Court rejected a claim of qualified immunity and made clear that no case on point is required in order to hold a government officer liable.

A victory in the Supreme Court for a civil rights plaintiff in a qualified immunity case is notable. Obviously, it is not possible at this time to know whether *Taylor* is only an aberration because of extreme facts or, alternatively, the beginning of a new approach to qualified immunity that is more amicable to civil rights plaintiffs. The Court's approach certainly is likely to matter in lower court litigation.

All government officials, when sued for money damages over constitutional violations, have an immunity defense.[2] State and local officials alleged to violate the Constitution can be sued under 42 U.S.C. § 1983. Section 1983 does not mention any defenses; it seemingly is written in absolute language. Under its terms, any state or local official who violates the Constitution can be sued for an injunction or for money. But the Supreme Court, in a series of cases largely beginning in the Burger Court era, has said that *all* government officials who are sued for money damages have an immunity defense.

The Supreme Court ruled that some government officials have absolute immunity and cannot be sued at all, no matter how malicious or egregious their constitutional violations. The Court has held that absolute immunity exists for judges performing judicial tasks, legislators performing legislative actions, prosecutors performing prosecutorial duties, law enforcement personnel testifying as witnesses, and the President of the United States for acts taken while carrying out the responsibilities of the presidency.

All other government officers have what is called "qualified immunity" when sued for money damages. The Court articulated the test for qualified immunity in 1982 in *Harlow v. Fitzgerald*.[3] In that case, the Court said that "[g]overnment officials performing discretionary functions, generally are shielded from liability for civil damages insofar as their conduct does not violate clearly established statutory or constitutional rights of which a reasonable person would have known."[4]

In 2011, in *Ashcroft v. al-Kidd*, the Court modified the phrasing of the *Harlow* test for qualified immunity.[5] The Court declared: "A Government official's conduct violates clearly established law when, at the time of the challenged conduct, '[t]he contours of [a] right [are] sufficiently clear' that *every 'reasonable official* would [have understood] that what he is doing violates that right.' We do not require a case directly on point, but existing precedent *must have placed the statutory or constitutional question beyond debate*."[6] Justice Scalia concluded his opinion by broadly defining the protection of qualified immunity. He wrote: "Qualified immunity gives government officials breathing room to make reasonable but mistaken judgments about open legal questions. When properly applied, it protects 'all but the plainly incompetent or those who knowingly violate the law.'"[7]

The Court has been very protective of defendants and expansive in defining qualified immunity. There have been 33 Supreme Court cases concerning qualified immunity since *Harlow v. Fitzgerald* and 30 of them have held in favor of the defendant government official. *Taylor v. Riojas* is only the third to rule in favor of a plaintiff.

Facts of *Taylor v. Riojas*

Taylor v. Riojas has appalling, disturbing facts. Trent Taylor is a prisoner in Texas. For a period of six days, he was confined in a pair of what the Court rightly described as "shockingly unsanitary cells."[8] The Court explained that "[t]he first cell was covered, nearly floor to ceiling, in 'massive amounts' of feces: all over the floor, the ceiling, the window, the walls, and even 'packed inside the water faucet.'"[9] Over a period of four days, Taylor could not eat or drink for fear of contamination.

Taylor was then moved to a very cold cell, "with only a clogged drain in the floor to dispose of bodily wastes."[10] The Court said: "Taylor held his bladder for over 24 hours, but he eventually (and involuntarily) relieved himself, causing the drain to overflow and raw sewage to spill across the floor. Because the cell lacked a bunk, and because Taylor was confined without clothing, he was left to sleep naked in sewage."[11]

Taylor sued the corrections officers, alleging that they violated the Eighth Amendment because their treatment of him was cruel and unusual punishment. The district court ruled in favor of the defendants based on qualified immunity, holding that they could not be held liable because they did not violate clearly established law that every reasonable officer should know.

The United States Court of Appeals for the Fifth Circuit affirmed the dismissal of Taylor's case.[12] Although the Court of Appeals concluded that Taylor's constitutional rights had been violated—confinement in these cells constituted cruel and unusual punishment—it also concluded that the officers were protected by qualified immunity. It said that the officers could not be held liable that because "[t]he law wasn't clearly established" that "prisoners couldn't be housed in cells teeming with human waste" for only six days.[13]

The Court's Decision

In a 7–1 decision, with only Justice Thomas dissenting (and Justice Barrett not participating), the Court reversed the Fifth Circuit in a *per curiam* opinion. The Court held that the officers were not protected by qualified immunity because "no reasonable correctional officer could have concluded that, under the extreme circumstances of this case, it was constitutionally permissible to house Taylor in such deplorably unsanitary conditions for such an extended period of time."[14] The Court said: "Confronted with the particularly egregious facts of this case, any reasonable officer should have realized that Taylor's conditions of confinement offended the Constitution."[15]

Justice Thomas did not write a dissenting opinion. The *per curiam* opinion simply states, "Justice Thomas dissents."[16]

Why It Matters

In recent years, the Supreme Court has expanded the protection of officers under qualified immunity. It has repeatedly stressed the need for a plaintiff to show a case on point in order to establish liability. In one of its most recent formulations of qualified immunity, *District of Columbia v. Wesby* in 2018, the Court was emphatic in how difficult it is for a plaintiff to succeed.[17] The Court stated:

> *[E]xisting law must have placed the constitutionality of the officer's conduct "beyond debate." This demanding standard protects "all but the plainly incompetent or those who knowingly violate the law." To be clearly established, a legal principle must have a sufficiently clear foundation in then-existing precedent. The rule must be "settled law," which means it is dictated by "controlling authority" or "a robust 'consensus of cases of persuasive authority.'" It is not enough that the rule is suggested by then-existing precedent. The precedent must be clear enough that every reasonable official would interpret it to establish the particular rule the plaintiff seeks to apply.*[18]

In case after case, the Supreme Court found officers were protected by qualified immunity under this standard.[19] Thus, the Court's ruling for the plaintiff in *Taylor v. Riojas* by denying qualified immunity is remarkable in that it is a striking departure from the norm.

But the Court's reasoning also is potentially quite significant. The Court, in its *per curiam* opinion, relies on two prior decisions: *United States v. Lanier*[20] and *Hope v. Pelzer*.[21] These are cases where the Court said that there does not have to be a prior decision on point to overcome qualified immunity.

United States v. Lanier, in 1997, was not a civil suit under § 1983, but rather was a criminal prosecution under 18 U.S.C. § 242. Both § 1983 and § 242 were enacted as part of the Civil Rights Act of 1871; the former creates civil liability and the latter criminal liability for those acting under color of state law who deprive a person of rights protected by the Constitution.

Lanier involved a state court judge who had sexually assaulted and harassed women in his chambers. The United States Court of Appeals for the Sixth Circuit ruled in favor of Lanier, emphasizing the absence of prior decisions explicitly deeming such conduct to be a violation of constitutional rights. The Supreme Court reversed and stressed that a reasonable person surely would know that such behavior is a violation of a woman's constitutional rights.

In *Hope v. Pelzer*, in 2002, a prisoner was tied to a hitching post as punishment and left in the hot sun for many hours. The Eighth Circuit found this to be cruel and unusual punishment, but said that the prison guards were protected by qualified immunity because there was not a prior decision that held the use of a hitching post as punishment was unconstitutional. The Supreme Court reversed, ruling that the defendants were not entitled to qualified immunity.

The Court, in an opinion by Justice Stevens, held that the key inquiry is whether the officer had "fair notice" that the conduct was a violation of rights. Justice Stevens explained that the central question in determining whether the prison officials could be held liable to Hope was "whether the state of the law in 1995 gave [them] fair warning that their alleged treatment of Hope was unconstitutional."[22] The Court explained: "Although earlier cases involving 'fundamentally similar' facts can provide especially strong support for a conclusion that the law is clearly established, they are not necessary to such a finding."[23] Rather, a plaintiff can overcome qualified immunity by showing that the reasonable officer under the circumstances should have known that the conduct was wrongful. The Court then reviewed the law as it existed in 1995 and said that the officers had fair warning that their conduct was unconstitutional.

But in the almost two decades since *Hope v. Pelzer*, the Court has repeatedly backed away from its approach, stressing the absence of cases on point as a basis for dismissing a case based on qualified immunity. The Court did not overrule or attempt to distinguish *Hope v. Pelzer*; rather, the Court simply abandoned *Hope*.

Taylor v. Riojas is extraordinary in that it reaffirms *Hope v. Pelzer*. The Court ruled that there does not need to be a case on point for a plaintiff to prevail and overcome qualified immunity.

Conclusion

In recent years, the Court's qualified immunity decisions have come under sharp criticism by liberal and conservative judges and commentators alike.[24] A team from Reuters won a Pulitzer Prize in 2021 for a series of articles documenting how qualified immunity prevents victims of police misconduct from successfully suing in court.[25] Proposals have been introduced into Congress to modify the law in this area. Perhaps *Taylor v. Riojas* is a response to that criticism and will lead to a Court that will be more willing to rule for plaintiffs when qualified immunity is at issue. Or maybe the case is just a reflection of truly horrific facts surrounding Taylor's confinement, and *Taylor v. Riojas* will be no more than an outlier in the Court's qualified immunity decisions. No matter how the Court proceeds from here on out, *Taylor* is an important ruling that has the potential to matter greatly in lower court litigation. *Taylor* reaffirms that there does not have to be a prior precedent on point to overcome qualified immunity and that all that is necessary for liability is that the officer had fair warning that the conduct was unconstitutional. It makes clear that *Hope v. Pelzer* remains good law.

Endnotes

1. 141 S. Ct. 52 (2020) (per curiam).
2. I review the law of immunity in detail in ERWIN CHEMERINSKY, FEDERAL JURISDICTION, ch. 8 (8th ed. 2019).
3. 457 U.S. 800 (1982).
4. *Id.* at 818.
5. 563 U.S. 731 (2011).
6. *Id.* at 741 (emphasis added) (citations omitted).
7. *Id.* at 743.
8. Taylor v. Riojas, 141 S. Ct. 52, 53 (2020) (per curiam).
9. *Id.*
10. *Id.*
11. *Id.*
12. Taylor v. Stevens, 946 F.3d 211 (2019).
13. *Id.* at 222.
14. 141 S. Ct. at 53.
15. *Id.* at 54.
16. *Id.*
17. 138 S. Ct. 577 (2018).
18. *Id.* at 589–90 (citations omitted).
19. *See, e.g.*, Wood v. Moss, 572 U.S. 744 (2014); Lane v. Franks, 573 U.S. 228 (2014); Brosseau v. Haugen, 543 U.S. 194 (2004).
20. 520 U.S. 259 (1997).
21. 536 U.S. 730 (2002).
22. *Id.* at 741.
23. *Id.*
24. *See, e.g.*, William Baude, *Is Qualified Immunity Unlawful*, 106 CALIF. L. REV. 45 (2018); Jay Schweikert, Qualified Immunity: A Legal, Practical, and Moral Failure, CATO INSTITUTE (2020), https://doi.org/10.36009/PA.901.
25. Andrew Chung et. al., *Supreme Defense*, REUTERS, May 8, 2020, https://www.reuters.com/investigates/special-report/usa-police-immunity-scotus/; Andrew Chung et. al., *Wrong Place, Wrong Time*, REUTERS, Aug. 25, 2020, https://www.reuters.com/investigates/special-report/usa-police-immunity-variations/; Lawrence Hurley et. al., *Dueling Rights*, REUTERS, Nov. 20, 2020, https://www.reuters.com/investigates/special-report/usa-police-immunity-guns/; Andrea Januta et. al., *Color of Suspicion*, REUTERS, Dec. 23, 2020, https://www.reuters.com/investigates/special-report/usa-police-immunity-race/.

5

Criminal Law and Criminal Procedure

As always, the Court decided a number of important cases concerning aspects of criminal law and procedure. I focus on three areas in this chapter. First, there were two cases that involved application of precedent, one concerning sentences for juvenile offenders and the other concerning whether the Court's recent decision requiring unanimous jury verdicts applies retroactively. I consider them together because looked at that way they are very revealing of the Court's approach to *stare decisis*. Second, there were three decisions concerning the Fourth Amendment and police searches and seizures. And finally, there were several rulings about specific federal criminal statutes.

Precedent and the Roberts Court

How much weight does the Roberts Court give to precedent? This is the crucial underlying question now that the Court has granted review in *Dobbs v. Jackson's Women's Health Organization*,[1] which puts the fate of *Roe v. Wade* before the justices.[2] The case concerns a Mississippi law that prohibits abortions after the fifteenth week of pregnancy and will be heard by the Court in the Fall of 2021.

Two cases decided by the Court during October Term 2020 involved the question of the justices' fidelity to precedent. The issue in *Jones v. Mississippi* was what must be demonstrated to impose a life sentence without parole for a murder committed by a juvenile.[3] In 2012, in *Miller v. Alabama*, the Court held that there cannot be a mandatory sentence of life without parole for a homicide committed by a juvenile.[4] In *Montgomery v. Louisiana*,[5] in 2016, the Supreme Court held that this applies retroactively to those who received such sentences prior to *Miller.*

Brett Jones was convicted of murdering his grandfather; Jones was 15 when the murder occurred. He was given a mandatory sentence of life without parole and challenged this in light of *Miller v. Alabama* and *Montgomery v. Louisiana*. He argued to the Court that there must be a finding of "incorrigibility" to justify such a sentence for a homicide committed by a juvenile. The Court, in a 6–3 decision, rejected this argument. Justice Kavanaugh wrote the majority opinion and declared that *Miller* only "required that a sentencer consider youth as a mitigating factor when deciding whether to impose a life-without-parole sentence. *Miller* did not require the sentencer to make a separate finding of permanent incorrigibility before imposing such a sentence."[6] The Court said that a punishment of life without parole for a homicide committed by a juvenile is allowed so long as "the sentence is not mandatory and the sentencer therefore has discretion to impose a lesser punishment."[7]

But this then means that *Miller* accomplished little. Long before *Miller*, in *Stanford v. Kentucky* in 1989, the Court held that a court must consider youth as a mitigating factor in imposing sentences.[8] Justice Sotomayor, in a dissenting opinion in *Jones* that was joined by Justices Breyer and Kagan, said that the Court's ruling "guts" *Miller* and *Montgomery* because as the Court stated in *Montgomery*, "*Miller*'s essential holding is that a lifetime in prison is a disproportionate sentence for all but the rarest children, those whose crimes reflect 'irreparable corruption.'"[9] Simply put, *Miller* and *Montgomery* imposed great limits on the ability to impose life without parole for homicides committed by juveniles; the majority in *Jones* reinterprets the earlier decisions as requiring no more than that the youth of the offender be considered as a mitigating factor in sentencing. Justice Sotomayor lamented, "How low this Court's respect for *stare decisis* has sunk."[10]

In one sense this decision is not surprising. *Miller* was a 5–4 decision, with Justices Kennedy and Ginsburg in the majority. It built on the earlier rulings in *Roper v. Simmons*,[11] which held that it is cruel and unusual punishment to impose a death sentence for a crime committed by a juvenile, and *Graham v. Florida*,[12] which held that it violates the Eighth Amendment to impose a sentence of life without parole for a non-homicide crime committed by a juvenile. Both, too, were 5–4, with Kennedy and Ginsburg in the majority. Their replacements, Justices Kavanaugh and Barrett, voted the opposite way in *Jones* and along with the other four conservative justices created the majority to interpret *Miller* and *Montgomery* very narrowly.

The other recent decision where the Court considered *stare decisis* was *Edwards v. Vannoy*.[13] A year earlier, in *Ramos v. Louisiana*, the Supreme Court held that the Sixth Amendment requirement for a unanimous jury verdict applies in state courts.[14] Two states, Louisiana and Oregon, had allowed convictions by non-unanimous juries. The issue in *Edwards v. Vannoy* is whether the requirement for unanimous juries applies retroactively to those who were convicted by non-unanimous juries before the Court's decision in *Ramos*.

Teague v. Lane, in 1989, held that a Supreme Court decision applies retroactively in two circumstances.[15] One is if it puts a matter beyond the constitutional reach of the criminal law; in other words, a substantive change in the law that limits what the government can punish applies retroactively. In *Montgomery v. Louisiana*, the Supreme Court made this explicit and stated: "[C]ourts must give retroactive effect to new substantive rules of constitutional law. Substantive rules include 'rules forbidding criminal punishment of certain primary conduct,' as well as 'rules prohibiting a certain category of punishment for a class of defendants because of their status or offense.'"[16]

The other circumstance where *Teague* held that a decision applies retroactively is a "watershed" rule of criminal procedure. It would seem that if anything is a watershed rule of criminal procedure, it would be the Court's decision in *Ramos*. In that decision, the Court said that a non-unanimous verdict "[i]s no verdict at all," and described the Sixth Amendment right to a unanimous jury "vital," "essential," "indispensable," and "fundamental" to the American legal system. [17]

But the Court, in a 6–3 decision in *Edwards v. Vannoy*, explicitly overruled that aspect of *Teague* and held that no longer is there an exception to allow retroactivity for watershed rules of criminal procedure. Justice Kavanaugh, again writing for the majority, declared, "New procedural rules do not apply retroactively on federal collateral review. The watershed exception is moribund. It must be regarded as retaining no vitality."[18]

Justice Kagan wrote a dissent joined by Justices Breyer and Sotomayor and lamented the disregard for *stare decisis*: "In overruling a critical aspect of *Teague*, the majority follows none of the usual rules of *stare decisis*. It discards precedent without a party requesting that action. And it does so with barely a reason given, much less the 'special justification' our law demands."[19]

In one sense, it is important not to overstate the significance of this ruling. Since *Teague*, never had the Court found anything to be a "watershed" rule of criminal procedure. Justice Kavanaugh stressed this in his majority opinion. But the explicit overruling of precedent and the Court's holding that a procedural rule will *never* apply retroactively are quite important.

As mentioned, both of these decisions were 6–3, with Roberts, Thomas, Alito, Gorsuch, Kavanaugh, and Barrett as the majority. No one should be surprised to see this split with great frequency in important cases on the current Court.

Several times in the past few years, the Court, in 5–4 decisions (with Ginsburg still on the Court and joining Breyer, Sotomayor, and Kagan in dissent) has expressly overruled precedent. In 2019, in *Franchise Tax Board v. Hyatt* (which I should disclose I argued on the losing side), the Court overruled the 40-year-old precedent of *Nevada v. Hall* and held that a state could not be sued in another state's court.[20]

Also, in 2019, in *Knick v. Township of Scott, Pennsylvania*,[21] the Court overruled its 1985 decision in *Williamson County Regional Planning Comm'n v. Hamilton Bank of Johnson City*, which held that a claim that property had been taken without just compensation could not be brought until state procedures had been exhausted.[22]

In 2018, in *Janus v. American Federation*,[23] the Court overruled its 1978 decision in *Abood v. Detroit Board of Education*, which held that the government could require non-union members to pay the share of the union dues that go to support its collective bargaining activities.[24] The conclusion is inescapable that precedent is given little weight in the Roberts Court.

The Fourth Amendment

The Court decided three cases concerning the Fourth Amendment during October Term 2020. They shared several characteristics. First, the police lost all of them, which is unusual for a Court that generally has sided with law enforcement in search and seizure cases. Second, none brought about a significant change in the law of the Fourth Amendment, though each provided a clarification that is sure to be important in some cases. And third, the Court repeatedly engaged in lengthy examination of the common law as of 1791 in deciding the meaning of the Fourth Amendment today. It certainly shows the influence of having several originalist justices and provides an important lesson to lawyers briefing and arguing cases before the Court.

The Supreme Court often has stressed the special protection for the home under the Fourth Amendment. Police generally need a warrant before entering and searching a person's dwelling. But this is not an absolute requirement; there are several exceptions to the warrant requirement. Two of the cases this term involved exceptions to the warrant requirement to searches for homes.

One exception is if the police are in "hot pursuit" of a person suspected of a crime. In cases such as *Warden v. Hayden* and *Payton v. New York* the Court expressly recognized that police may enter a home without a warrant if they are chasing someone suspected of a crime.[25] But what if the person being pursued is suspected of committing a misdemeanor crime?

That was the issue in *Lange v. California*.[26] Arthur Lange was repeatedly honking his horn while driving with the radio blaring. Such excessive noise is a misdemeanor in California. A police officer observed this and put the lights on his car to pull Lange over. But Lange went into his driveway and garage. The officer got out of his car and went into the garage. He saw that Lange was intoxicated and arrested him for driving under the influence.

Lange argued that the officer violated the Fourth Amendment by entering the garage without a warrant. The officer argued that it was permissible because he was in hot pursuit. The lower courts sided with the police and found no violation of the Fourth Amendment.

The Supreme Court reversed in an opinion by Justice Kagan. The Court, though, refused to create a bright-line rule that hot pursuit never justifies warrantless entry when the crime is a misdemeanor. Instead, the Court said that it will require a case-by-case analysis and that warrantless entry when there is hot pursuit of a misdemeanor case would be justified if there is the risk of destruction of evidence or of flight or of imminent harm to others.

In fact, the Court went so far as to say that this "approach will in many, if not most, cases allow a warrantless home entry."[27] But the Court expressly rejected a rule that would have allowed entry without a warrant whenever there is hot pursuit in a misdemeanor case. Justice Kagan wrote that "the need to pursue a misdemeanant does not trigger a categorical rule allowing home entry, even absent a law enforcement emergency."[28] Justice Kagan justified this conclusion, in part, on a detailed examination of the common law as of 1791 when the Fourth Amendment was adopted.

The other case involving exceptions to the warrant requirement was *Caniglia v. Strom*.[29] A married couple got into an argument. The woman left the house and stayed in a hotel that night. She was afraid that her husband might have harmed himself when she could not reach him by phone. She called the police. They found the man at home and he was fine. Nonetheless, the police took him into custody for a mental health evaluation. The police later returned to the home without a warrant and seized his guns.

The man sued the police for violating his Fourth Amendment rights. The officers defended by saying that their actions were justified by a "community caretaking" exception to the warrant requirement. The First Circuit sided with the police. The Supreme Court, though, reversed in a unanimous opinion by Justice Thomas. In one of the shortest majority opinions of the year, the Court made clear that community caretaking is a very narrow exception that has no application to searches of people's homes.

The community caretaking exception to the warrant requirement comes from *Cady v. Dombrowski*, in 1973.[30] An off-duty police officer, Dombrowski, was arrested for driving while intoxicated and his car was towed to a police lot. The arresting officer thought that Dombrowski's service revolver still might be in the car and went and searched the vehicle. In the search of the car, the officer found evidence that tied Dombrowski to a murder. This was the crucial evidence that led to Dombrowski's conviction.

The Supreme Court, 5–4, concluded that the search of the car without a warrant did not violate the Fourth Amendment and that therefore the evidence gained was admissible. The Court invoked the automobile exception to the warrant requirement. But the Court also stressed that the police did not violate the Fourth Amendment because they were involved in "community caretaking."

Since *Cady v. Dombrowski*, there has been confusion in the lower courts about this exception and when it applies. In *Caniglia v. Strom*, the Court made clear that it has no application to searches of homes. Justice Thomas declared: "What is reasonable for vehicles is different from what is reasonable for homes. *Cady* acknowledged as much, and this Court has repeatedly 'declined to expand the scope of . . . exceptions to the warrant requirement to permit warrantless entry into the home.'"[31]

That seems simple and straightforward, but there is another exception to the warrant requirement when there are "exigent circumstances." The elimination of the community caretaking exception hardly seems to matter when police can engage in a warrantless search if they reasonably believe that there are exigent circumstances. The Court did not discuss whether these facts would be sufficient to constitute exigent circumstances and allow for a warrantless entry and search of the home.

When is a person seized by the police for purposes of the Fourth Amendment? In *United States v. Mendenhall*, in 1980, the Court said that a person is seized if a reasonable person in the circumstances "would have believed that he was not free to leave."[32] In *California v. Hodari D.*, in 1991, the Court ruled that the police chasing a suspect was not a seizure; the seizure occurred only once the person was tackled by the police officer.[33] The result was that evidence dropped by the person during the chase was admissible against him. Because the chase was not a search, no reasonable suspicion or probable cause was required for it.

Torres v. Madrid, decided this Term, again raised the question of whether a person had been seized.[34] Four New Mexico State Police officers arrived at an apartment complex in Albuquerque to execute an arrest warrant for a woman. Roxanne Torres lived in the complex and happened to be walking to her car when the police arrived. The officers decided to speak with Torres despite her not being a suspect in the case. The officers saw her get into her car and attempted to talk with her. Apparently, she did not notice them until one of them tried to open the door of her car. She thought the officers were carjackers trying to steal her car and she hit the gas to escape them.

The officers began shooting and fired 13 shots at Torres, striking her twice in the back and temporarily paralyzing her left arm. Torres drove through the bullets, exited the apartment complex, drove a short distance, and stopped in a shopping center parking lot. Torres saw an unoccupied car with its motor running. She stole the car and drove 75 miles to a hospital. The police arrested her the next day. She pleaded no contest to aggravated fleeing from a law enforcement officer, assault on a peace officer, and unlawfully taking a motor vehicle. But she sued the police officers for using excessive force.

In *Graham v. Connor*, in 1989, the Court held that excessive police force is a seizure that violates the Fourth Amendment.[35] But was Torres considered seized because she still was able to drive 75 miles? The Court ruled in her favor and held that "[t]he application of physical force to the body of a person with intent to restrain is a seizure, even if the force does not succeed in subduing the person."[36] Chief Justice Roberts wrote for the Court and said: "A seizure requires the use of force *with intent to restrain*. Accidental force will not qualify. Nor will force intentionally applied for some other purpose satisfy this rule."[37] Chief Justice Roberts justified this conclusion, in part, on a careful look at the common law before 1791.

Justice Gorsuch wrote a vehement dissent, joined by Justices Thomas and Alito. He argued that the woman was not seized as evidenced by the fact that she drove 75 miles. He contended that a person is not seized until the police take possession of them.

As mentioned, *Torres v. Madrid* arose in the context of a civil suit for excessive police force. It is much harder to imagine the context in a criminal case, when there is a motion to suppress evidence, where this is likely to matter. *Hodari D.* remains the law: police chasing of a suspect is not a seizure for purposes of the Fourth Amendment.

The Court has developed an elaborate body of doctrines concerning the Fourth Amendment. They arise in countless cases, criminal and civil, every day. The three cases this term provide clarification about some aspects of the Fourth Amendment and are revealing of the Court's methodology, putting great emphasis on the common law rules as they existed in 1791.

Federal Criminal Law

As is true every year, a number of the cases this term involved issues of federal criminal law. Perhaps the most high profile of these was *Van Buren v. United States*, where the Court construed the federal Computer Fraud and Abuse Act.[38] The statute prohibits conduct that "exceeds authorized access" of a computer. Specifically, the statute defines tis as meaning "to access a computer with authorization and to use such access to obtain . . . information . . . that the accesser is not entitled so to obtain."

Nathan Van Buren, a Georgia police officer, took a bribe to run a license-plate check. As part of his job he was authorized to run license-plate checks, but not for illicit purposes. The lower courts upheld a conviction under the CFAA, concluding he was not entitled to check license-plate records for private purposes.

The Supreme Court, in a 6–3 decision, reversed. Justice Barrett wrote for the Court. Justice Thomas wrote the dissent, joined by Chief Justice Roberts and Justice Alito. The Court narrowly interpreted CFAA and held that it is a crime only if users access information they were not entitled to obtain.

Justice Barrett focused on the text of the statute, specifically the prohibition on obtaining information that "the accesser is not entitled *so* to obtain." Justice Barrett focused on the meaning of the word "so" and quoted Black's Law Dictionary, for the proposition that the word "so" is "a term of reference that recalls 'the same manner as has been stated.'"[39] The Court said that what the statute prohibits is obtaining "information one is not allowed to obtain *by using a computer that he is authorized to access.*"[40]

Justice Barrett noted that extending the statute to "every violation of a computer-use policy" would make criminals of "millions of otherwise law-abiding citizens," offering examples of such trivial conduct as "embellishing on online-dating profile" and "using a pseudonym on Facebook"—activities that violate website use restrictions and thus would fall within the government's understanding of the CFAA.[41] The bottom line is that the Court interprets the statute as applying only if users access information they were not entitled to obtain.

In *United States v. Briggs*, the defendants were charged in military court with committing rape.[42] Under the Uniform Code of Military Justice (UCMJ), any offense that potentially carries a death sentence is not subject to the five-year statute of limitations that applies to lesser crimes. Rape is categorized as a crime that may carry that sentence under the UCMJ. However, the Supreme Court has held that the Eighth Amendment bars capital punishment for rape.[43] Because rape no longer has the potential to carry a death sentence, the defendants argued that this means rape is subject to the five-year statute of limitations. For them, that would mean they could not be charged because the Government waited over five years to bring charges against them.

The Court, though, found that rape is considered a crime without a statute of limitations under the UCMJ. This is true although the UCMJ only refers to crimes "punishable by death" as having no statute of limitations and Court precedent has barred capital punishment for rape. The Court reasoned that the statute uses "punishable by death" only as a reference to a group of crimes that includes rape, so the fact that the statute is now factually inaccurate does not limit rape to a five-year statute of limitations. That means that the defendants could be charged and prosecuted for rape.

In *Borden v. United States*, the defendant was facing an enhanced sentencing under the Armed Career Criminal Act (ACCA) for unlawfully owning a gun.[44] The ACCA provides stricter punishments for defendants who have previously been convicted of three violent felonies. This was intended to target repeat offenders who are deemed "career criminals." The defendant had three prior felonies, but one of them was for a crime with a reckless mental state as the *mens rea* element. The defendant argued that because the *mens rea* was not intentional, this crime did not count as a "violent felony" under the Act and thus he was not eligible for enhanced sentencing.

The Court ruled in his favor and held that under the ACCA, an offense does not count as a qualifying violent crime for an enhanced punishment if that crime only includes recklessness as a *mens rea* element. The ACCA requires an offense to have an intentional *mens rea* to qualify as a violent crime under the Act. This was because the Act defined a violent crime as one that involved the "use of physical force against the person of another" and that "against" meant that a *mens rea* of purposefulness or knowledge was required. Thus, the defendant could not be sentenced under the ACCA.

In *Greer v. United States* (and its companion case, *United States v. Gary*), the trial court judges gave the juries the wrong instructions as to the mental state—the *mens rea*—required under a felon-in-possession statute that the defendants were being charged under. [45] Subsequently, the Supreme Court clarified the *mens rea* element for their offenses in *Rehaif v. United States*, holding that defendants must know they are felons to satisfy the mental state element of the crime.[46] After this, the defendants sought review of their sentences, arguing that the courts wrongly instructed them in their proceedings.

The Court held that the Federal Rules of Criminal Procedure require a defendant who had a *Rehaif* error in their case to show that it affected their substantial rights in order to be entitled to plain-error relief. For felon-in-possession cases, *Rehaif* errors are not grounds for plain-error relief unless defendants first made a sufficient argument on appeal that they would have presented evidence that they didn't know they were felons had they know about the *Rehaif* decision.

Simply asking for plain-error relief because the lower court made a mistake is not enough. Here, defendants did not show that the mistakes affected their substantial rights or significantly affected the outcome of the case. This is especially true considering both defendants had prior felonies and the Court did not believe they would not have been aware of their criminal status. This *mens rea* would have been easy for the Government to prove. Thus, the Court concluded that the defendants were not entitled to plain-error relief.

Finally, in *Terry v. United* States,[47] the defendant was convicted for a crack offense and sentenced based on a portion of the criminal statute that did not base the sentencing guideline on drug quantity and did not have a mandatory minimum sentence.[48] After Congress passed sentencing reform in the First Step Act of 2018, defendant sought a sentence reduction. However, it wasn't clear if the statute applied to his sentence because the reform was targeted to crack offenses based on provisions that carried a mandatory minimum sentence, which were (A) and (B) but not (C).

The Court held that crack offenders are eligible for sentence reduction under the First Step Act only if their crack offense triggered a mandatory minimum sentence punishment under federal law. In other words, crack offenders sentenced under 21 U.S.C. § 841(b)(1)(C) are *not* eligible for sentence reduction under the First Step Act. Because defendant's sentence was based on (C), he was not eligible for a sentence reduction.

Endnotes

1. Dobbs v. Jackson Women's Health, No. 19-1392, 2021 WL 1951792, at *1 (U.S. May 17, 2021).
2. Roe v. Wade, 410 U.S. 113 (1973).
3. Jones v. Mississippi, 141 U.S. 1307, (2021).
4. Miller v. Alabama, 567 U.S. 460 (2012).
5. Montgomery v. Louisiana, 577 U.S. 190 (2016).
6. *Jones*, 141 U.S. at 1316.
7. *Id.* at 1311.
8. Stanford v. Kentucky, 492 U.S. 361 (1989).
9. *Jones*, 141 U.S, at 1328.
10. *Id.* at 1336.
11. Roper v. Simmons, 543 U.S. 551 (2005).
12. Graham v. Florida, 560 U.S. 48 (2010).
13. Edwards v. Vannoy, 141 U.S. 1547 (2021).
14. Ramos v. Louisiana, 140 U.S. 1390 (2020).
15. Teague v. Lane, 489 U.S. 288 (1989).
16. 577 U.S. 190, 198 (2016).
17. 149 S. Ct. at 1396.
18. *Edwards*, 141 U.S. at 1560.
19. *Id.* at 1574.
20. Franchise Tax Bd. of Cal. v. Hyatt, 139 U.S. 1485 (2019).
21. Knick v. Township of Scott, 139 U.S. 2162 (2019).
22. Williamson Cnty. Reg'l Plan. Com'n v. Hamilton Bank, 473 U.S. 172 (1985).

23. Janus v. Am. Fed'n., 138 U.S. 2448 (2018).
24. Abood v. Detroit Bd. Of Ed., 431 U.S. 209 (1977).
25. Warden v. Hayden, 387 U.S. 294 (1967); Payton v. New York, 445 U.S. 573 (1980).
26. Lange v. California, 141 U.S. 2011 (2021).
27. *Id.* at 2021.
28. *Id.* at 2021–22.
29. Caniglia v. Strom, 141 U.S. 1596 (2021).
30. Cady v. Dombrowski, 413 U.S. 433 (1973).
31. *Strom*, 141 U.S. at 1600.
32. United States v. Mendenhall, 446 U.S. 544, 554 (1980).
33. California v. Hodari D., 499 U.S. 621 (1991).
34. Torres v. Madrid, 141 U.S. 989 (2021).
35. Graham v. Connor, 490 U.S. 386 (1989).
36. *Torres*, 141 U.S. at 993.
37. *Id.* at 998.
38. 141 S. Ct. 1648 (2021).
39. *Id.* at 1654.
40. *Id.*
41. *Id.* at 1650.
42. United States v. Briggs, 141 U.S. 467 (2020).
43. Coker v. Georgia, 433 U.S. 584 (1977).
44. Borden v. United States, 141 U.S. 1817 (2021).
45. Greer v. United States, 141 U.S. 2090 (2021).
46. Rehaif v. United States, 139 U.S. 2191 (2019).
47. Terry v. United States, 141 U.S. 1858 (2021).
48. *Id.* at 1862; *see also* 21 U.S.C. § 841(b)(1)(C) (2018).

6

Federal Jurisdiction

The Supreme Court long has been clear that Article III of the Constitution limits who has standing to sue in federal court. For a plaintiff to have standing, the Constitution requires that the plaintiff demonstrate an injury that was caused by the defendant and that is likely to be remedied by a favorable court decision.

Standing to sue in federal court was addressed by the Supreme Court in a number of cases in the 2020 October Term.[1] One of the most important rulings of the term was *California v. Texas*, which dismissed a challenge to the Patient Protection and Affordable Care Act (ACA) because of a lack of standing.[2] The Court also narrowed the ability to use congressional statutes as the basis for standing in *TransUnion, LLC v. Ramirez*.[3] But in *Uzuegbunam v. Preczewski*, the Court held that a request for nominal damages satisfies the redressability element necessary for Article III standing where a plaintiff's claim is based on a completed violation of a legal right.[4]

California v. Texas

The Supreme Court's decision to dismiss the challenge to the Patient Protection and Affordable Care Act broke no new legal ground. Despite this, it has enormous practical significance in that it means that 21 million people will keep their health insurance coverage.

In 2012, in *National Federation of Independent Business v. Sebelius*, the Court in a 5–4 decision upheld the constitutionality of the Affordable Care Act (also known as Obamacare).[5] One of the key issues before the Court was the constitutionality of the individual mandate that required people to purchase insurance or pay a penalty. The Court, in an opinion by Chief Justice Roberts, held that the individual mandate was a valid exercise of Congress's power to impose a tax for the general welfare.

The Affordable Care Act created many new restrictions on insurance companies to protect consumers: it prohibited medical insurance companies from denying coverage because of preexisting conditions, it stopped insurers from charging higher premiums to those with chronic conditions, and it eliminated caps on yearly or lifetime benefits. The ACA's individual mandate was crucial for these reforms because it prevented people from only purchasing insurance after they became sick. Without exclusions for preexisting conditions, people might wait to get health insurance until they were ill. If people could freely do that, the health insurance market would become flooded with a pool of only sick patients. This would undermine the viability of the market because health insurance works only if coverage includes healthy people to defray the cost of insuring the ill.

In December 2017, as part of the Tax Cuts and Jobs Act of 2017, Congress eliminated the individual mandate by setting the penalty amount at $0 for individuals not purchasing health insurance.[6] The requirement for having insurance still existed, but there were no consequences for refusing to enroll in a healthcare plan.

Texas, along with about a dozen other States and two individuals, brought suit against federal officials claiming that without the penalty, the ACA's minimum essential coverage provision is unconstitutional. They argued that the individual mandate had been upheld as a tax, but no longer could be characterized in that manner because Congress had eliminated the penalty for failing to purchase health insurance. Texas argued that this made the entire Act unconstitutional. The Trump administration agreed with the challengers and urged the federal court to strike down the entire healthcare statute. California and other "blue" states intervened to defend the law.

A federal district court agreed with the challengers that the individual mandate was unconstitutional and that this likely made the entire Act unconstitutional. The United States Court of Appeals for the Fifth Circuit, in a 2–1 decision, agreed that the individual mandate no longer was constitutional, but remanded the case to consider whether this provision could be severed from the rest of the statute or whether it made the whole law invalid. Before the district court could consider the issue, the Supreme Court granted certiorari on three questions: (1) Do the plaintiffs have standing to challenge the individual mandate? (2) If so, is the individual mandate unconstitutional? (3) If it is unconstitutional, is it severable from the rest of the statute?

The Supreme Court focused on only the first question. In a 7–2 decision, the Court dismissed the case for lack of standing. Justice Breyer wrote the opinion for the Court and said that none of the plaintiffs have shown an injury "fairly traceable" to the "allegedly unlawful conduct" that has been challenged.[7] The individual plaintiffs could not show any injury because, without a penalty for noncompliance, the Act is unenforceable. Thus, they could not show any injury resulting from the Affordable Care Act that would give them standing to sue in court.

Likewise, the Court said that Texas and the other states failed to demonstrate any monetary injuries as a result of the ACA's individual mandate penalty of $0. There was no showing that the change in federal law would cause more people to enroll in the program and thus increase their costs. Nor had the states shown that their direct increase in administrative costs were a result of the change in the law.

Justice Alito, joined by Justice Gorsuch, dissented. Alito said: "The ACA imposes many burdensome obligations on States in their capacity as employers, and the 18 States in question collectively have more than a million employees. Even $1 in harm is enough to support standing. Yet no State has standing? In prior cases, the Court has been generous in allowing States to sue."[8]

Justice Alito argued that once the individual mandate penalty was reduced to zero, it could no longer be justified as a tax. Because the individual mandate could not be separated from the rest of the law, finding the provision unconstitutional meant that the remainder of the ACA was no longer enforceable. In other words, these two justices would have declared the entire Affordable Care Act unconstitutional.

It is crucial to remember that everything about the Affordable Care Act has been deeply partisan. Every Republican in Congress voted against it. Four conservative justices would have struck down the entire law in 2012. At the time, conservative law professor Amy Coney Barrett was outspoken in criticizing the Supreme Court when it upheld the law. Texas and other "red" states, in tandem with the Trump administration, saw this suit as their best chance to finally kill the law. And conservative judges in the lower courts went along with their objective.

The Supreme Court's decision in *California v. Texas* will likely end serious legal challenges to the Affordable Care Act in the future. Although it has not fulfilled all of its promises, the ACA has been a clear success. It is no longer as politically controversial as when it was initially adopted. And the stakes in the third round of challenges to the ACA could not have been higher. The United States is in the midst of the worst public health crisis in over a century. Today, over 20 million Americans receive their health insurance through the Affordable Care Act. Undoubtedly, the justices were cognizant of the issues at stake when they heard the case and issued their firm ruling to uphold the Act. The case is enormously important for what the Court did not do: it did not strike down the Affordable Care Act.

TransUnion LLC v. Ramirez

The Supreme Court long has said that Congress can create rights by statute, albeit ones that would not otherwise exist, and the infringement of those rights constitutes a sufficient injury for standing. The Court has explained that "Congress may create a statutory right or entitlement the alleged deprivation of which can confer standing to sue even where the plaintiff would have suffered no judicially cognizable injury in the absence of statute."[9] But in *TransUnion LLC v. Ramirez*, the Court significantly limited Congress's power to do this.

The Fair Credit Reporting Act regulates the consumer reporting agencies that compile and disseminate personal information about consumers. The law requires that consumer reporting agencies "follow reasonable procedures to assure maximum possible accuracy" in consumer reports.[10] It provides that consumer reporting agencies must disclose to consumers all information in their file at the time of request. The Act also compels reporting agencies to "provide to a consumer, with each written disclosure by the agency to the consumer," a "summary of right" prepared by the Consumer Financial Protection Bureau.[11] Importantly for this case, the Act creates a cause of action for consumers to sue and recover damages for certain violations.

The Court initially addressed standing under this law in *Spokeo, Inc. v. Robin* in 2016.[12] Spokeo owned and operates a website that provides in-depth reports containing personal information about individuals. Thomas Robins alleged that his Spokeo profile was filled with inaccuracies, including about his employment, his marital status, and whether he had children. Robins sued Spokeo for violating the Fair Credit Reporting Act.[13] The law, among other things, authorizes victims of "willful" violations to recover statutory damages of "not less than $100 and not more than $1,000."[14]

The issue before the Court was whether Robins had standing to sue. The Ninth Circuit held that Robins had standing because Congress, created a right by statute, and the infringement of that statutory right was sufficient for standing. But the Supreme Court, in a 6–2 decision, reversed and remanded the case. Notably, the Court did not change the law. It reaffirmed that Congress, by statute, can create rights the infringement of which is sufficient for standing to sue in federal courts. The Court approvingly quoted Justice Kennedy's concurring opinion in *Lujan v. Defenders of Wildlife* that "Congress has the power to define injuries and articulate chains of causation that will give rise to a case or controversy where none existed before."[15]

But the Court, in an opinion by Justice Alito, said that in order to have an injury sufficient for standing it must be "particularized" and "concrete."[16] This, of course, is familiar language that has appeared in many Supreme Court cases about standing. The difference here, though, is that never before had the Court treated these as two distinct requirements. The Court said that "[f]or an injury to be 'particularized,' it 'must affect the plaintiff in a personal and individual way,'" and the Court found that Robins met this requirement.[17]

The Court, however, said that a particularized injury is not sufficient for standing; it also must be a "concrete harm" and the Ninth Circuit had not considered whether the injury was "concrete." The issue for this case on remand, and for all other civil litigation in federal courts, is what it meant for an injury to be "concrete." The Court said:

> *"[C]oncrete" injury must be "de facto"; that is, it must actually exist. When we have used the adjective 'concrete,' we have meant to convey the usual meaning of the term—"real," and not "abstract." Concreteness, therefore, is quite different from particularization. "Concrete" is not, however, necessarily synonymous with "tangible." Although tangible injuries are perhaps easier to recognize, we have confirmed in many of our previous cases that intangible injuries can nevertheless be concrete.*[18]

The Court said that in deciding whether an intangible injury is concrete, "both history and the judgment of Congress play important roles. Because the doctrine of standing derives from the case-or-controversy requirement, and because that requirement in turn is grounded in historical practice, it is instructive to consider whether an alleged intangible harm has a close relationship to a harm that has traditionally been regarded as providing a basis for a lawsuit in English or American courts."[19]

But this definition of "concrete" gives little guidance to lower courts. Moreover, though the Court says that being "particularized" and "concrete" are distinct requirements that must be met in order for there to be an injury sufficient for standing, the difference between these two requirements is unclear. My students read Justice Alito's language and were perplexed by his definition of concrete.

The Court returned in 2021 to the issue of standing under the Fair Credit Reporting Act in *TransUnion LLC v. Ramirez*.[20] TransUnion is a credit reporting agency that compiles personal and financial information about individuals and creates consumer reports that are sold to entities that request information about the credit of consumers. In 2002 TransUnion introduced an add-on product called OFAC Name Screen Alert. When a business opted into OFAC, TransUnion would conduct its credit check and use a third-party software to compare a consumer's name against a list maintained by the United States Department of Treasury's Office of Foreign Assets Control (OFAC). Hence the OFAC add-on. This list contained the OFAC's known terrorists, drug traffickers, and other serious criminals. If a consumer's first and last name matched a first and last name of someone on OFAC's list, then TransUnion would place an alert on the report to indicate a consumer was a potential "match" to an OFAC name. TransUnion at the time did not compare any data other than first and last names.

Sergio Ramirez learned the hard way that he is one of these individuals. Ramirez visited a car dealership in 2013 to purchase a vehicle. His credit check at the dealer returned an OFAC advisor alert. Due to matching on the terror list, the dealer refused to sell to Ramirez. Ramirez then called TransUnion to request a copy of his credit file, which was mailed to him. However, the first mailing did not include the OFAC alert, and the second mailing with the OFAC alert did not include a summary of his rights.

A class action suit was brought on behalf of 8,185 individuals with OFAC alerts in their credit files, including Ramirez, against TransUnion under the Fair Credit Reporting Act for failing to use reasonable procedures to ensure their credit files were accurate. The three claims included reputational harm based on these inaccurate credit files and two claims relating to formatting defects in mailings sent by TransUnion to the class members. Prior to trial, only 1,853 members had their misleading reports with OFAC alerts provided to third parties during the seven-month time period. The internal credit files of the rest of the 6,332 class members were not provided to third parties during that time period.

The Supreme Court ruled that this group lacked standing to sue, notwithstanding the federal law creating such a right and authorizing suits. The Court reiterated that, to have Article III standing to sue in federal court, plaintiffs must demonstrate that they suffered a "concrete" harm. The Court emphasized that a concrete harm is assessed based on whether it has a "close relationship" to a harm traditionally recognized as providing a basis for a lawsuit in American courts. The Court declared:

> *What makes a harm concrete for purposes of Article III? As a general matter, the Court has explained that "history and tradition offer a meaningful guide to the types of cases that Arti-*

> *cle III empowers federal courts to consider." And with respect to the concrete-harm requirement in particular, this Court's opinion in Spokeo v. Robins indicated that courts should assess whether the alleged injury to the plaintiff has a "close relationship" to a harm "traditionally" recognized as providing a basis for a lawsuit in American courts. That inquiry asks whether plaintiffs have identified a close historical or common-law analogue for their asserted injury.*[21]

The Court then spoke of the role of Congress in creating rights that are the basis for standing:

> *In determining whether a harm is sufficiently concrete to qualify as an injury in fact, the Court in Spokeo said that Congress's views may be "instructive." Courts must afford due respect to Congress's decision to impose a statutory prohibition or obligation on a defendant, and to grant a plaintiff a cause of action to sue over the defendant's violation of that statutory prohibition or obligation. In that way, Congress may "elevate to the status of legally cognizable injuries concrete, de facto injuries that were previously inadequate in law." But even though "Congress may 'elevate' harms that 'exist' in the real world before Congress recognized them to actionable legal status, it may not simply enact an injury into existence, using its lawmaking power to transform something that is not remotely harmful into something that is." Importantly, this Court has rejected the proposition that "a plaintiff automatically satisfies the injury-in-fact requirement whenever a statute grants a person a statutory right and purports to authorize that person to sue to vindicate that right."*[22]

The Court, in a 5–4 decision, applied this to hold that members of the class whose false credit reports had not been circulated lacked standing to sue. Justice Kavanaugh wrote the opinion for the Court, joined by Chief Justice Roberts and Justices Alito, Gorsuch, and Barrett. The Court said that Ramirez did not suffer a harm with a close relationship to those harms traditionally recognized as providing a basis for a lawsuit.

Justice Thomas wrote a dissent joined by Justices Breyer, Sotomayor, and Kagan. It is not a combination of justices that has been seen very often. Justice Thomas argued that the violation of a statutory right is sufficient for standing: "[S]tatutes create legal rights, the invasion of which creates standing. And this understanding accords proper respect for the power of Congress and other legislatures to define legal rights . . . In light of the history, tradition, and common practice, our test should be clear: So long as a statute fixes a minimum of recovery, . . . there would seem to be no doubt of the right of one who establishes a technical ground of action to recover this minimum sum without any specific showing of loss."[23]

Thomas noted that "[n]ever before has this Court declared that legal injury is *inherently* insufficient to support standing. And never before has this Court declared that legislatures are constitutionally precluded from creating legal rights enforceable in federal courts if those rights deviate too far from their common-law roots."[24]

Justice Kagan wrote a separate dissent, joined by Justices Breyer and Sotomayor. She echoed the key point in Justice Thomas's dissent: never before had the Court limited standing to sue to enforce a statutory right based on whether it is one that existed at common law. She wrote: "The Court here transforms standing law from a doctrine of judicial modesty into a tool of judicial aggrandizement. It holds, for the first time, that a specific class of plaintiffs whom Congress allowed to bring a lawsuit cannot do so under Article III."[25]

TransUnion LLC v. Ramirez limits the ability to sue to enforce federal statutes creating rights. The Court's emphasis on the common law in determining whether it is a cognizable injury is a significant restriction on standing. For example, in *Trafficante v. Metropolitan Life Insurance*, the Court allowed standing to enforce the Fair Housing Act based on it seeing Congress as creating a right to interracial association.[26] But there was no such common law right.

Or consider standing to sue under the federal Freedom of Information Act. It creates a statutory right to all documents possessed by the federal government unless they fit into one of nine categories of exceptions. It authorizes standing to sue when documents are withheld. It is a statute that creates a right, albeit a right that did not exist at common law. After the Court's decision in *TransUnion* is such standing allowed to enforce this statute?

The requirement for injury under Article III has been created and enforced only in the last half century. Why should the common law be used to define something that did not exist then? There is no doubt that this case will cause great confusion over what federal laws creating rights can be enforced in the federal courts.

Uzuegbunam v. Preczewski

Is a claim for nominal damages sufficient for standing? In *Uzuegbunam v. Preczewski*, the Court, in an 8–1 decision, said yes.[27]

The case was brought by two students at Gwinnett College, a public university in Georgia, who wished to exercise their religion by sharing their faith on campus while enrolled as students. In 2016, Uzuegbunam talked with interested students and handed out religious literature on campus grounds. Uzuegbunam was stopped by a campus police officer who informed Uzuegbunam that campus policy prohibited distributing religious materials outside of areas that are designated free speech zones. A college official then confirmed that the policy allowed religious speech and distributing religious materials in designated speech areas on campus. However, when Uzuegbunam obtained permits and tried to speak again in a free speech zone, a campus police officer stopped him again and informed him that other students were complaining about his speech. The officer told Uzuegbunam that his speech had violated campus policy because it led to complaints. Uzuegbunam complied with the order and stopped speaking. Joseph Bradford, another Gwinnett College student who shared Uzuegbunam's faith, decided not to speak about religion because of these events.

Both students sued the college officials charged with enforcement of the college's speech policies, claiming that the policies violated the First Amendment. The students sought injunctive relief and nominal damages. The college ultimately decided to alter and discontinue the challenged policies rather than defend them, and they sought to dismiss the lawsuit on the ground that the policy change left the students without standing to sue. The parties agreed the policy change made the students' injunctive argument moot but disputed whether the students had standing to maintain the suit for their nominal damages claim.

The Court, in an opinion by Justice Thomas, said that the request for nominal damages satisfies the redressability element necessary for Article III standing where a plaintiff's claims is based on a completed violation of a legal right. Justice Thomas said, "In determining whether nominal damages can redress a past injury, we look to the forms of relief awarded at common law."[28] The Court said that the prevailing rule at common law was that a party whose rights are invaded can always recover nominal damages without evidence of actual damages. Plaintiffs were permitted to pursue nominal damages whenever they suffered a personal legal injury, regardless of the size of the economic rights.

The Court stressed that a request for redress in the form of nominal damages does not guarantee standing. Redressability must be coupled with an establishment of other elements of standing and the plaintiffs must satisfy all other requirements such as pleading a cognizable cause of action. But the Court said that Uzuegbunam suffered a violation of his constitutional rights to free speech when the college enforced their speech polices against him. Nominal damages can redress his injury even if he cannot or chooses not to quantify that harm.

Chief Justice Roberts was the sole dissenter in *Uzuegbunam*. I cannot think of another instance where Roberts was alone in a dissent. He argued that the case is moot and cannot be saved by a claim for nominal damages. Roberts pointed out that not only did the two students no longer attend Gwinnett College, but also that the challenged restrictions no longer existed. The petitioners also did not allege actual damages, so the case is moot because a federal court cannot grant "any effectual relief whatever."[29] Nominal damages do not alleviate the harms suffered by a plaintiff, nor are they intended to. Roberts expressed concern that "[i]f nominal damages can preserve a live controversy, then federal courts will be required to give advisory opinions whenever a plaintiff tacks on a request for a dollar."[30] He accused the majority of "turning judges into advice columnists."[31]

Although the majority phrased its holding in terms of standing, it is easier to understand the case with regard to mootness. Because a claim for nominal damages is sufficient to meet the constitutional standing requirements it also keeps a case from being moot.

Conclusion

It is difficult to generalize from these cases. Perhaps the most that can be said is that in the realm of federal jurisdiction, like other areas of constitutional law, the Supreme Court is focusing on common law as of the time the Constitution was written. The 2020 Term shows the impact of originalists on the Court. The turn in focus toward an original understanding of standing is odd: since standing, and the specific requirements for it, did not exist back then, it is unclear why the common law of 1787 should be given so much emphasis.

Endnotes

1. In addition to the cases discussed in this chapter, the Court also dismissed two other cases for lack of standing. In *Trump v. New York*, 141. S. Ct. 530 (2020) (per curiam), the Court, 6–3, held that the plaintiffs lacked standing to challenge the constitutionality of the President's memorandum directing exclusion of undocumented citizens from apportionment bases for congressional apportionment from the census. The Court said that any injury to the plaintiff was too speculative. In *Carney v. Adams*, 141 S. Ct. 493 (2020), the Court dismissed for lack of standing a challenge to a Delaware law that required political balance on the courts. The Supreme Court said that the plaintiff lacked standing because Adams did not show that he was "able and ready" to apply for a judicial vacancy in the imminent future, and therefore failed to show a personal concrete and imminent injury necessary for Article III standing.

2. 141 S. Ct. 2104 (2021).

3. 141 S. Ct. 2190 (2021).

4. 141 S. Ct. 792 (2021).

5. 567 U.S. 519 (2012).

6. CCH Legislative Documents, Treaties (CCH) P P.L. 115-97, § 11081; Eileen Sullivan and Michael Tackett, *President Signs Bill into Law, and Seems to Ask for a Pat on the Back*, N.Y. Times, Dec. 23, 2017, at A15.

7. 141 S. Ct. at 2113.
8. 141 S. Ct. at 2124 (Alito, J., dissenting).
9. Warth v. Seldin, 422 U.S. 490, 514 (1975).
10. 15 U.S.C. § 1681e(b).
11. 15 U.S.C. § 1681g(c)(2).
12. 136 S. Ct. 1540 (2016).
13. Fair Credit Reporting Act of 1970 (FCRA or Act), 84 Stat. 1127, as amended, 15 U.S.C. § 1681 *et seq*.
14. 15 U.S.C. § 1681n(a)(1)(A).
15. 136 S. Ct. at 1549.
16. *Id.* at 1548.
17. *Id.* at 1548.
18. *Id.* at 1548–49.
19. *Id.* at 1549.
20. 141 S. Ct. 2190 (2021).
21. 141 S. Ct. at 2204 (citations omitted).
22. 141 S. Ct. at Id. (citations omitted).
23. 141 S. Ct. at 2218 (Thomas, J., dissenting) (citations omitted) (quotations omitted).
24. *Id.* at 2221 (Thomas, J., dissenting).
25. *Id.* at 2225 (Kagan, J., dissenting).
26. Trafficante v. Metro. Life Ins. Co., 409 U.S. 205 (1972).
27. 141 S. Ct. 792 (2021).
28. *Id.* at 797-98.
29. *Id.* at 803 (Roberts, C.J., dissenting) (quoting another source).
30. *Id.* at 803 (Roberts, C.J., dissenting).
31. *Id.* at 804.

7

First Amendment: Free Exercise of Religion

Of all the areas of constitutional law, the place where dramatic change is most likely because of the new composition of the Court is with regard to the religion clauses of the First Amendment.[1] Indeed, the clearest manifestation of the effects of replacing Justice Ginsburg with Justice Barrett was seen in cases involving free exercise challenges to restrictions imposed to stop the spread of COVID-19. More generally, the conservative majority of the Court is aggressively protecting free exercise of religion.

This was evident in several decisions a year ago, during October Term 2019. *Espinoza v. Montana Department of Revenue* involved a Montana law that allowed parents sending their children to private school to receive a $150 tax credit.[2] In Montana, almost all of the private schools are religious. The Montana Supreme Court invalidated the tax credit law as violating the Montana state constitution which forbids direct or indirect government aid to religion.

But the Supreme Court, 5–4, concluded that the Montana Supreme Court violated free exercise of religion in invalidating the Montana program. Chief Justice John Roberts wrote the opinion for the Court and said that the Montana constitution prevented parents from receiving aid if they sent their children to religious as opposed to secular private schools. This, the Court concluded, violated free exercise of religion. The Court said that the government must have a compelling reason and no other alternative any time it denies benefits to religious institutions that it allows to secular ones.

The practical effect of this decision, which follows from the Court's ruling in *Trinity Lutheran of Columbia, Missouri v. Comer* in 2017,[3] is that whenever the government gives benefits to secular private schools it must provide them to religious schools unless it can be shown that doing so would violate the Establishment Clause of the First Amendment. Prior to *Trinity Lutheran*, never had the Court found that the Free Exercise Clause *required* the government provide aid to religious institutions.

Also, in 2020, in *Our Lady of Guadalupe School v. Morrissey-Berru*, the Court held that a religious school cannot be held liable under employment discrimination laws for the choices it makes as to its teachers.[4] In *Hosana-Tabor Lutheran Evangelical School v. EEOC* (2012), the Court concluded that a fifth-grade teacher who had been ordained as a minister in the faith could not sue a religious school for employment discrimination.[5]

In *Our Lady of Guadalupe School*, the Court in a 7–2 decision, with Justice Alito writing the majority, held that religious schools are exempt from employment discrimination laws for the choices they make as to their teachers. This means that religious schools are free to discriminate on the basis of race, sex, religion, sexual orientation, age, and disability in hiring and firing teachers.

Finally in 2020, in *Little Sisters of the Poor Saint Peters and Paul Home v. Pennsylvania*, the Court upheld the authority of the Trump administration under the Affordable Care Act to promulgate rules exempting employers with religious or moral objections from providing contraceptive coverage to their employees.[6]

This trend of the Court expanding the protections of the Free Exercise Clause was evident in October Term 2020 in the justices upholding religious challenges to restrictions imposed to stop the spread of COVID and in *Fulton v. City of Philadelphia.*

Religious Challenges to COVID Restrictions

A number of cases have come to the Court involving religious challenges to restrictions imposed to lessen the spread of COVID-19. These have come to the Court on its so-called "shadow docket." These are matters that come to the Court for emergency relief, usually to grant or to stay an injunction. They do not have the usual briefing and oral argument seen in the "merits cases," which are all of the others discussed in this book.

There is a dramatic difference in how the Court handled these religious challenges to COVID restrictions with Justice Ginsburg as opposed to Justice Barrett on the bench. The first of these came to the Court in May 2020, *South Bay Pentecostal Church v. Newsom.*[7] California Governor Gavin Newsom, as part of his order to limit the spread of COVID-19, restricted attendance at religious worship services to 25% of building capacity or 100 attendees, whichever is lower. A church in Southern California sued to enjoin this as infringing its free exercise of religion.

The federal district court and the United States Court of Appeals for the Ninth Circuit ruled against the church. They sought an injunction from the Supreme Court. The Court, in a 5–4 ruling also denied an injunction. The majority was Roberts, Ginsburg, Breyer, Sotomayor, and Kagan. There was no opinion for the Court, but Roberts wrote an opinion just for himself. He rejected the government's claim that there had been discrimination against religion: "Although California's guidelines place restrictions on places of worship, those restrictions appear consistent with the Free Exercise Clause of the First Amendment. Similar or more severe restrictions apply to comparable secular gatherings, including lectures, concerts, movie showings, spectator sports, and theatrical performances, where large groups of people gather in close proximity for extended periods of time. And the Order exempts or treats more leniently only dissimilar activities, such as operating grocery stores, banks, and laundromats, in which people neither congregate in large groups nor remain in close proximity for extended periods."[8]

Roberts expressed the need for great deference to the actions of government officials taken to limit the spread of COVID and said:

> *Our Constitution principally entrusts "[t]he safety and the health of the people" to the politically accountable officials of the States "to guard and protect." When those officials "undertake[ ] to act in areas fraught with medical and scientific uncertainties," their latitude "must be especially broad." Where those broad limits are not exceeded, they should not be subject to second-guessing by an "unelected federal judiciary," which lacks the background, competence, and expertise to assess public health and is not accountable to the people.*[9]

Justice Kavanaugh wrote a dissent joined by Justices Thomas and Gorsuch. (Justice Alito also dissented but did not write an opinion). Justice Kavanaugh, in a preview of what was to come in later cases, stressed that he saw Governor Newsom's order as discriminating against religion. He said that the "safety guidelines discriminate against places of worship and in favor of comparable secular businesses. Such discrimination violates the First Amendment."[10] He said that the "basic constitutional problem is that comparable secular businesses are not subject to a 25% occupancy cap, including factories, offices, supermarkets, restaurants, retail stores, pharmacies, shopping malls, pet grooming shops, bookstores, florists, hair salons, and cannabis dispensaries."[11]

This was the central question as the Court dealt with this issue in subsequent cases: should religious gatherings be compared to secular gatherings that are seen as comparable in their likelihood of spreading COVID-19? Or should religious gatherings be compared to the most leniently regulated secular activities?

This was the question again in July 2020, when the Court ruled in *Calvary Chapel Dayton Valley v. Sisolak.*[12] Nevada Governor Steve Sisolak imposed restrictions to limit the spread of COVID that included not allowing more than 50 people at a religious service. A church sued for an injunction and the district court and the court of appeals denied it. Once more the Supreme Court also denied an injunction by a 5–4 margin, again with Roberts, Ginsburg, Breyer, Sotomayor, and Kagan as the majority. None wrote an opinion and there was no opinion for the Court.

Justice Alito wrote for the four dissenters. It was an angry, sarcastic dissenting opinion that stressed the view that religious entities were being discriminated against. He wrote:

> *The Constitution guarantees the free exercise of religion. It says nothing about the freedom to play craps or blackjack, to feed tokens into a slot machine, or to engage in any other game of chance. But the Governor of Nevada apparently has different priorities. Claiming virtually unbounded power to restrict constitutional rights during the COVID–19 pandemic, he has issued a directive that severely limits attendance at religious services. . . . That Nevada would discriminate in favor of the powerful gaming industry and its employees may not come as a surprise, but this Court's willingness to allow such discrimination is disappointing. We have a duty to defend the Constitution, and even a public health emergency does not absolve us of that responsibility.*[13]

The Court returned to this issue on November 25, 2020, releasing an opinion shortly before midnight on the day before Thanksgiving. *Roman Catholic Diocese of Brooklyn v. Cuomo* involved restrictions imposed by New York Governor Andrew Cuomo to limit the spread of COVID-19.[14] Governor Cuomo's order categorized areas of the state based on the prevalence of COVID. In the areas most afflicted, "red zones," no more than 10 persons could attend each religious service, and in "orange zones," attendance was capped at 25. Catholic churches and Orthodox Jewish synagogues in Brooklyn sought an injunction. As in the prior two cases, and relying on them, the district court and the United States Court of Appeals for the Second Circuit denied injunctions.

But the Supreme Court, 5–4, granted the application for injunctive relief. There was a *per curiam* opinion, joined by Justices Thomas, Alito, Gorsuch, Kavanaugh, and Barrett. The majority stressed, as did the dissenters in the two prior cases, that the Governor's order discriminated against religion. The Court stated:

> *In a red zone, while a synagogue or church may not admit more than 10 persons, businesses categorized as "essential" may admit as many people as they wish. And the list of 'essential' businesses includes things such as acupuncture facilities, campgrounds, garages, as well as many whose services are not limited to those that can be regarded as essential, such as all plants manufacturing chemicals and microelectronics and all transportation facilities. The disparate treatment is even more striking in an orange zone. While attendance at houses of worship is limited to 25 persons, even non-essential businesses may decide for themselves how many persons to admit.*[15]

The Court said that because the Governor's order discriminated against religion, it had to meet strict scrutiny. The Court concluded that it was likely to fail this test and that therefore the injunction was to be granted. The Court declared:

> *But even in a pandemic, the Constitution cannot be put away and forgotten. The restrictions at issue here, by effectively barring many from attending religious services, strike at the very heart of the First Amendment's guarantee of religious liberty. Before allowing this to occur, we have a duty to conduct a serious examination of the need for such a drastic measure.*[16]

Justice Gorsuch wrote a separate concurring opinion to even more emphatically declare that the restrictions on religious worship violated the First Amendment. He began by stating:

> *Government is not free to disregard the First Amendment in times of crisis. At a minimum, that Amendment prohibits government officials from treating religious exercises worse than comparable secular activities, unless they are pursuing a compelling interest and using the least restrictive means available.*

> *Yet recently, during the COVID pandemic, certain States seem to have ignored these long-settled principles.*[17]

Justice Gorsuch explicitly rejected the deference to the government that Chief Justice Roberts had urged in the earlier case.

Four justices dissented and there were three dissenting opinions. Chief Justice Roberts' dissent focused on mootness: the churches and synagogues that brought the challenge were in areas that already had been reclassified to allow greater attendance.

Justice Breyer, joined by Justices Sotomayor and Kagan, dissented and stressed the dangers of COVID and the number who had died and become ill from it. He argued for deference to government officials to stop the spread of the deadly disease.

Justice Sotomayor, joined by Justice Kagan dissented, and disagreed that there was any discrimination against religion. She said that religious entities were treated the same as comparable secular ones. She concluded her dissent:

> *Free religious exercise is one of our most treasured and jealously guarded constitutional rights. States may not discriminate against religious institutions, even when faced with a crisis as deadly as this one. But those principles are not at stake today. The Constitution does not forbid States from responding to public health crises through regulations that treat religious institutions equally or more favorably than comparable secular institutions, particularly when those regulations save lives. Because New York's COVID–19 restrictions do just that, I respectfully dissent.*[18]

What is the difference between this case and the two prior ones that came to an opposite conclusion? It is not factual distinctions or different legal principles. The prior two cases were 5–4 rulings with Justice Ginsburg in the majority. This case was 5–4, but with Justice Barrett joining the dissenters from the earlier two cases to create the majority.

This was seen again in April 2021 in *Tandon v. Newsom.*[19] The restrictions imposed by California Governor Gavin Newsom limited the number of households that could gather in any home. The regulation said that no more than three households of people could gather in a home and it did not distinguish between secular and religious activities. It did not matter whether people were gathering to watch to Super Bowl or for a book club or to worship. Plaintiffs, who wanted to gather in a home for religious worship, sought an injunction. Like in the earlier cases, the district court and the court of appeals ruled against them.

The Supreme Court, 5–4, said that the request for an injunction should be granted. Again, the majority was Justices Thomas, Alito, Gorsuch, Kavanaugh, and Barrett. The *per curiam* opinion was even more emphatic about the need to treat religion the same as the most leniently regulated comparable secular activity. The Court declared:

> *[G]overnment regulations are not neutral and generally applicable, and therefore trigger strict scrutiny under the Free Exercise Clause, whenever they treat any comparable secular activity more favorably than religious exercise. It is no answer that a State treats some comparable secular businesses or other activities as poorly as or even less favorably than the religious exercise at issue.*[20]

The Court said that Governor's order, because of its discrimination against religion, had to meet strict scrutiny and that it failed this test.

The Court also said that

> *even if the government withdraws or modifies a COVID restriction in the course of litigation, that does not necessarily moot the case. And so long as a case is not moot, litigants otherwise entitled to emergency injunctive relief remain entitled to such relief where the applicants "remain under a constant threat" that government officials will use their power to reinstate the challenged restrictions.*[21]

The decision says that Chief Justice Roberts would deny the request for an injunction, but he did not write an opinion. Justice Kagan wrote a strong dissent joined by Justices Breyer and Sotomayor. She said that religious gatherings were treated the same as secular ones and that is all the First Amendment requires. She said the "law does not require that the State equally treat apples and watermelons."[22]

Justice Kagan explained why the distinctions drawn by the Governor's order makes sense:

> *First, when people gather in social settings, their interactions are likely to be longer than they would be in a commercial setting, with participants more likely to be involved in prolonged conversations. Second, private houses are typically smaller and less ventilated than commercial establishments. And third, social distancing and mask-wearing are less likely in private settings and enforcement is more difficult. These are not the mere musings of two appellate judges: The district court found each of these facts based on the uncontested testimony of California's public-health experts.*[23]

This case, like *Roman Catholic Diocese of Brooklyn*, reflects the importance of the change in the composition of the Court. It also reflects a crucial difference between the majority and the dissent as to analysis under the Free Exercise Clause. The majority says that religion must be treated as favorably as the most leniently regulated secular activity. The dissent says that religion cannot be discriminated against as compared to similar secular activities. There is no doubt that the five most conservative justices are seeking to provide much greater protection for religion and religious gatherings. Perhaps, too, there is a difference on the Court between conservatives and liberals, just as there is in American society, about the need for government regulations to stop the spread of COVID.

Fulton v. City of Philadelphia[24]

The City of Philadelphia contracts with private social service agencies to help place children in foster homes. Private foster care agencies are "delegated" the power of the government in determining whether individuals satisfy the state-law requirements for becoming foster parents. Every contract is explicit in prohibiting the agency from discriminating on the basis of race, sex, religion, and sexual orientation.

Catholic Social Services long had participated in this aspect of the program, but in recent years has declined to do so because of the contractual requirement that it not discriminate based on sexual orientation. Catholic Social Services says that its religious beliefs prevent it from providing inspections or placing children with same sex-couples.

Catholic Social Services challenged the non-discrimination requirement as violating its First Amendment rights. The district court and the United States Court of Appeals for the Third Circuit rejected these arguments. Both courts relied on the Supreme Court's 1990 decision in *Employment Division v. Smith*, which held that free exercise of religion does not provide a basis for an exemption from a general government law.[25] In an opinion by Justice Antonin Scalia, the Court rejected a claim by Native Americans that they should be granted an exemption from a state law prohibiting consumption of peyote on account of their religious beliefs. The Court held that the Free Exercise Clause cannot be used to challenge a neutral law of general applicability.

In *Fulton*, the Supreme Court unanimously reversed the lower courts and ruled in favor of Catholic Social Services. Chief Justice Roberts wrote the opinion for the Court. He said that under *Employment Division v. Smith* a "law is not generally applicable if it 'invite[s]' the government to consider the particular reasons for a person's conduct by providing a mechanism for individualized exemptions."[26] The Philadelphia ordinance gave city officials the authority to grant exceptions to the non-discrimination requirement. The Court said that it was irrelevant that none ever had been granted and that there was no evidence of discrimination against religious entities. The existence of discretion was enough for it to not be a neutral law of general applicability. Therefore, it had to meet strict scrutiny.

The Court concluded that the City failed to meet strict scrutiny and that its policy was therefore unconstitutional: "The refusal of Philadelphia to contract with CSS for the provision of foster care services unless it agrees to certify same-sex couples as foster parents cannot survive strict scrutiny, and violates the First Amendment."[27]

Justice Alito concurred in the judgment, joined by Justices Thomas and Gorsuch. In a 77-page opinion, Justice Alito expressly called for the Court to overrule *Employment Division v. Smith.* Justice Alito argued at length against the *Smith* approach and stated:

> *We should reconsider without further delay. The correct interpretation of the Free Exercise Clause is a question of great importance, and Smith's interpretation is hard to defend. It can't be squared with the ordinary meaning of the text of the Free Exercise Clause or with the prevalent understanding of the scope of the free-exercise right at the time of the First Amendment's adoption. It swept aside decades of established precedent, and it has not aged well. Its interpretation has been undermined by subsequent scholarship on the original meaning of the Free Exercise Clause. Contrary to what many initially expected, Smith has not provided a clear-cut rule that is easy to apply, and experience has disproved the Smith majority's fear that retention of the Court's prior free-exercise jurisprudence would lead to "anarchy."*[28]

Justice Gorsuch wrote a separate opinion concurring in the judgment criticizing the Court's majority for not reconsidering and overruling *Smith.*

Justice Barrett wrote a concurring opinion which was joined in full by Justice Kavanaugh. She expressed agreement with many of the criticisms of *Smith* advanced by Justice Alito. She wrote:

> *I find the historical record more silent than supportive on the question whether the founding generation understood the First Amendment to require religious exemptions from generally applicable laws in at least some circumstances. In my view, the textual and structural arguments against Smith are more compelling. As a matter of text and structure, it is difficult to see why the Free Exercise Clause—lone among the First Amendment freedoms—offers nothing more than protection from discrimination.*[29]

But she said that there are hard questions as to what test should replace the one from *Employment Division v. Smith.* She said that the Court did not need to address that in this case because the City of Philadelphia policy was unconstitutional "regardless whether *Smith* stays or goes."[30]

What does the case mean? First, the future of *Employment Division v. Smith* is in doubt; three justices call for it to be overruled and two others express support for that view. But the more *Smith* is eroded and especially if it is overruled, courts will face the enormously difficult task of defining religion and determining what is a sincerely held religious belief. *Smith* made those issues largely irrelevant because religion was not given an exemption from general laws.

Second, although the Court did not overrule *Smith*, it did substantially restrict its scope. The repeated statements in the media that the Supreme Court's decision in *Fulton v. City of Philadelphia* was a narrow ruling are wrong. The Court said that any law that burdens religion and gives *any* discretion to government officials must meet strict scrutiny.

Third, ultimately, the underlying question is whether religious beliefs provide an exemption from a government law prohibiting discrimination. This was the issue, albeit in a different context, in *Masterpiece Cakeshop v. Colorado Civil Rights Commission* in 2018.[31] That case involved a baker who refused to design and bake a cake for a same-sex wedding in violation of a Colorado law that prohibited business establishments from discriminating based on sexual orientation. That case, too, involved both claims of free exercise of religion and freedom of speech. The Supreme Court did not resolve these issues, instead finding that hostility to religion had been expressed in the Colorado Civil Rights Commission and that this violated free exercise of religion.

But there are many cases raising the same issue involving florists, photographers, and stationery stores which refuse to serve same-sex couples on account of the business owner's religious beliefs. The issue also is sure to arise in light of the Supreme Court's ruling in June in *Bostock v. Clayton County, Georgia*, which held that Title VII of the 1964 Civil Rights Act prohibits employment discrimination on the basis of sexual orientation or gender identity.[32] Justice Gorsuch's majority opinion expressly left open the issue of whether an employer's religious beliefs provide a basis for discriminating against gay, lesbian, or transgender individuals.

The underlying ultimate issue is one of profound importance. There inherently is a tension between liberty and equality. Any law that prohibits discrimination limits the freedom to discriminate. For over a half century, the Supreme Court has found stopping discrimination to be more important than protecting a right to discriminate. *Fulton* indicates that the Court is likely to say that upholding religious freedom is more important than protection from discrimination.

Endnotes

1. *See* HOWARD GILLMAN & ERWIN CHEMERINSKY, THE RELIGION CLAUSES: THE CASE FOR SEPARATING CHURCH AND STATE (Geoffrey R. Stone, et. al, eds., 2020).
2. Espinoza v. Montana Dep't. of Revenue, 140 S. Ct. 2246 (2020).
3. Trinity Lutheran Church of Columbia, Inc. v. Comer, 137 S. Ct. 2012 (2017).
4. Our Lady of Guadalupe Sch. v. Morrissey-Berru, 140 S. Ct. 2049 (2020).
5. Hosanna-Tabor Evangelical Lutheran Church & Sch. v. E.E.O.C., 565 U.S. 171 (2012).
6. Little Sisters of the Poor Saints Peter & Paul Home v. Pennsylvania, 140 S. Ct. 2367 (2020).
7. South Bay United Pentecostal v. Newsom, 140 S. Ct. 1613 (2020).
8. *Id.* at 1613 (Roberts, C.J., concurring).
9. *Id.* at 1613–14.
10. *Id.* at 1614 (Kavanaugh, J., dissenting)
11. *Id.*
12. Calvary Chapel Dayton Valley v. Sisolak, 140 S. Ct. 2603 (2020).
13. *Id.* at 2603–04 (Alito, J., dissenting).
14. Roman Catholic Diocese of Brooklyn v. Cuomo, 141 S. Ct. 63 (2020).
15. *Id.* at 66.
16. *Id.* at 68.
17. *Id.* at 69 (Gorsuch, J., concurring).
18. *Id.* at 81.
19. Tandon v. Newsom, 141 S. Ct. 1294 (2021).
20. *Id.* at 1296.
21. *Id.* at 1297.
22. *Id.* at 1298.
23. *Id.*
24. Fulton v. Phila., 141 S. Ct. 1868 (2021).
25. Emp. Div., Dept. of Human Resources of Or. v. Smith, 494 U.S. 872 (1990).
26. *Fulton*, 141 S. Ct. at 1878.
27. *Id.* at 1882.
28. *Id.* at 1888 (Alito, J., concurring in the judgment).

29. *Id.* at 1882 (Barrett, J., concurring).
30. *Id.* at 1883.
31. Masterpiece Cakeshop v. Colo. C.R. Com'n., 138 S. Ct. 1719 (2018).
32. Bostock v. Clayton County, 140 S. Ct. 1731 (2020).

8

First Amendment: Freedom of Speech

For much of the twentieth century there was a clear liberal/conservative divide on speech. Liberals were advocates of more protection of speech; conservatives often favored greater restrictions. This was evident in First Amendment issues like whether the government can regulate obscenity and when people can be punished for incitement. But now, the ideological division is often less clear. There are times when conservatives are more aggressive in calling for speech protection, such as in wanting to strike down restrictions on campaign spending.[1] But there also are times when conservatives favor more regulation of speech than liberals, such as in holding that the First Amendment provides no protection for the speech of government employees on the job in the scope of their duties.[2]

There were two free speech decisions by the Supreme Court in October Term 2020. One case, about student speech, was nearly unanimous. The other, about a First Amendment right to anonymity for contributions to non-profit organizations, was divided along ideological lines.

Mahanoy Area School District v. B.L.

Brandi Levy made the Mahoney Area High School junior varsity cheerleading team as a freshman. She tried out for the varsity team as a sophomore, but again was assigned to the junior varsity squad. She was especially upset because an incoming freshman made the varsity.

On Saturday, from off campus, Levy posted two messages on Snapchat. These messages were visible on Snapchat for 24 hours. Her first message consisted of a photo in which she and a classmate raised their middle fingers at the camera, with the caption: "Fuck school fuck softball fuck cheer fuck everything." Levy's second message, posted shortly thereafter, consisted of complaining that she and another student were on junior varsity again, but did not contain any profanities.

The coaches determined that Levy's posts "could impact students in the school," and had violated team rules that Levy had agreed to follow, including that cheerleaders should "have respect for [their] school, coaches, teachers, [and] other cheerleaders" and avoid "foul language and inappropriate gestures." The coaches removed Levy from the cheer team for the school year, but informed Levy that she could try out again as a rising junior. No other disciplinary action was taken.

Levy and her parents sued in federal district court, which granted a preliminary injunction reinstating her to the team and then summary judgment in her favor. The United States Court of Appeals for the Third Circuit affirmed, stressing that schools cannot punish off-campus speech. In *Tinker v. Des Moines Independent Community School District*,[3] the Court ruled that schools can punish speech if there is a substantial disruption of school activities. The Third Circuit, though, said that *Tinker* "does not apply to off-campus speech," to "speech that is outside school-owned, -operated, or -supervised channels and that is not reasonably interpreted as bearing the school's imprimatur." The majority elaborated that schools cannot invoke *Tinker* even to address "off-campus student speech threatening violence or harassing particular students or teachers."[4]

There only have been a handful of Supreme Court decisions dealing with the issue of student speech. In *Tinker v. Des Moines Independent Community School District*, the Court said that the First Amendment protected the ability of students in a high school to wear black armbands to protest the Vietnam War.[5] In an opinion by Justice Fortas, the Court said that "[i]t can hardly be argued that either students or teachers shed their constitutional rights to freedom of speech or expression at the schoolhouse gate."[6] The Court said that "[i]n our system, state-operated schools may not be enclaves of totalitarianism. School officials do not possess absolute authority over their students. . . . [Students] are possessed of fundamental rights which the State must respect."[7] The Court said that speech is protected absent a showing that it would "materially and substantially interfere with the requirements of appropriate discipline in the operation of the school."[8]

In subsequent years, however, the Court has been much less protective of speech in school environments and much more deferential to school authorities. In *Bethel School District No. 403 v. Fraser*, the Court upheld the punishment of a student for a speech given at a school assembly, nominating another student for a position in student government, that was filled with sexual innuendo.[9] The speaker was suspended for a few days and kept from delivering an address at his graduation. The Court upheld the punishment and emphasized the need for judicial deference to educational institutions.

The Court went even further in its deference to school authorities in *Hazelwood School District v. Kuhlmeier*.[10] A school newspaper produced as part of a journalism class was going to publish, with the approval of its faculty advisor, stories about three students' experience with pregnancy and about the impact of divorce on students. No students' names were included in the article on pregnancy, and one was mentioned in the article on divorce (although the name had been deleted after the paper had been forwarded to the principal for review). The principal decided to publish the paper without these articles by deleting the two pages on which they appeared. The principal expressed the view that the articles on pregnancy discussed sexual activity and birth control in a manner that was inappropriate for some of the younger students at the school, that the three students in the article on pregnancy might be identified from other aspects of the article, and that the parents of the student identified in the article about divorce should have the opportunity to respond. The Supreme Court upheld the principal's decision and rejected the First Amendment challenge. Justice

White concluded that the school newspaper was a nonpublic forum and that as a result "school officials were entitled to regulate the content of [the school newspaper] in any reasonable manner."

The most recent Supreme Court decision concerning student speech, 14 years ago, also evidenced great deference to school officials. In *Morse v. Frederick*, the Court held that the First Amendment was not violated when a student was punished for displaying a banner with the inscription, "Bong Hits 4 Jesus."[11] When the Olympic torch came through Juneau, Alaska, a high school released its students from class to watch as a student unfurled his banner. The principal, believing that the banner encouraged drug use, confiscated it and suspended the student who displayed it. In an opinion by Chief Justice John Roberts, the Court, in a 5–4 decision, said that the principal could reasonably interpret the banner as encouraging illegal drug use and that schools have an important interest in stopping such speech.

The issue before the Court in *Mahanoy School District v. B.L.* is how, if at all, these precedents apply to student off-campus speech over social media. The Supreme Court, in an 8–1 decision, ruled in favor of the student and against the school. Justice Breyer wrote the opinion for the Court and only Justice Thomas dissented. Justice Breyer was clear from the outset that the Court was holding that this student's speech was protected, but it was not going as far as the Third Circuit in concluding that schools never can punish off-campus speech. The Court left open the ability of schools to punish off-campus expression that involves bullying or harassment or cheating.

Justice Breyer explained that three factors mean that the school has less interest and ability to punish off-campus speech. "*First*, a school, in relation to off-campus speech, will rarely stand *in loco parentis*."[12] Parents, not the school, are generally responsible for behavior outside of school. "*Second*, from the student speaker's perspective, regulations of off-campus speech, when coupled with regulations of on-campus speech, include all the speech a student utters during the full 24-hour day."[13] The concern is with schools having the power to regulate what students do every minute of every day. "*Third*, the school itself has an interest in protecting a student's unpopular expression, especially when the expression takes place off campus. America's public schools are the nurseries of democracy."[14]

The more schools punish student speech, the more they are conveying a message that is inimical to the First Amendment.

Justice Breyer stressed that B.L.'s speech was critical of a school official; the core of the First Amendment long has been seen as safeguarding expression about the government and its officers. The Court rejected the school's claimed interest in teaching good manners or in upholding team morale. Likewise, the Court stressed that there was no evidence that Levy's speech was significantly disruptive of school activities.

Justice Breyer observed that, "It might be tempting to dismiss B. L.'s words as unworthy of the robust First Amendment protections discussed herein. But sometimes it is necessary to protect the superfluous in order to preserve the necessary."[15] Levy's speech was sophomoric, but she was a sophomore.

Importantly, the Court did not hold that schools never can punish off-campus speech. Justice Breyer's opinion was explicit in rejecting the Third Circuit's approach:

> *The school's regulatory interests remain significant in some off-campus circumstances. . . . These include serious or severe bullying or harassment targeting particular individuals; threats aimed at teachers or other students; the failure to follow rules concerning lessons, the writing of papers, the use of computers, or participation in other online school activities; and breaches of school security devices, including material maintained within school computers.*[16]

Justice Thomas was the lone dissent. His view is that students have no First Amendment rights that protect them from school discipline. He said that a "more searching review reveals that schools historically could discipline students in circumstances like those presented here."[17] Justice Thomas reviewed this history and chastised the majority for ignoring it.

Why does this case matter? It is the first case since *Tinker* in 1969 to rule in favor of the student and against the school in a speech case. It provides broad, though not absolute, protection for expression that occurs outside of school. Given the reality of modern communications, so many of the cases arising in the lower courts involve speech off-campus over social media. And the Court identifies the circumstances where schools can punish off-campus speech. It is an important decision in addressing an issue that will affect schools and students across the country.

Americans for Prosperity Foundation v. Bonta[18]

Under California law, the California Attorney General's Office is responsible for enforcing state laws regulating charitable fundraising. Under state law, the Attorney General is authorized to "establish and maintain a register" of charitable organizations and to obtain "whatever information, copies of instruments, reports, and records are needed for the establishment and maintenance of the register."[19]

The California Attorney General has required that charities, in renewing their registration with the state, file copies of their Internal Revenue Service Form 990, along with any attachments and schedules. Charities must file Form 990 with the federal government. Among other things it requires organizations to disclose the names and addresses of donors who have contributed more than $5,000 in a particular tax year. Conservative not-for-profit groups brought a challenge based on the First Amendment.

The issue before the Supreme Court was whether it violated freedom of association because of the possible chilling effect of disclosure for California to require that charities turn over to the State the document they already have to give to the federal government.

The Supreme Court in a 6–3 decision declared the California law unconstitutional. Chief Justice Roberts wrote an opinion that was joined in full by two justices (Kavanaugh and Barrett) and in part by three justices (Thomas, Alito, and Gorsuch). Although all six of these justices agreed that the law was unconstitutional, they disagreed as to the level of scrutiny to be applied. Chief Justice Roberts said that the test is "exacting scrutiny."[20] He wrote. "We have since settled on a standard referred to as 'exacting scrutiny.' Under that standard, there must be 'a substantial relation between the disclosure requirement and a sufficiently important governmental interest.' 'To withstand this scrutiny, the strength of the governmental interest must reflect the seriousness of the actual burden on

First Amendment rights.'"[21] The Court contrasted exacting scrutiny with strict scrutiny. It said: "Under strict scrutiny, the government must adopt "the least restrictive means of achieving a compelling state interest rather than a means substantially related to a sufficiently important interest. . . . While exacting scrutiny does not require that disclosure regimes be the least restrictive means of achieving their ends, it does require that they be narrowly tailored to the government's asserted interest."[22]

By contrast Justice Thomas concurred in the judgment and said that strict scrutiny should be used. Justice Alito, joined by Justice Gorsuch, concurred in the judgment and rejected needing to choose between strict scrutiny and exacting scrutiny. He wrote: "I am not prepared at this time to hold that a single standard applies to all disclosure requirements. And I do not read our cases to have broadly resolved the question in favor of exacting scrutiny."

Writing for the majority, Chief Justice Roberts said that there was no evidence that the disclosures to the Attorney General did anything to help regulate charities. He quoted the federal district court that there was not "a single, concrete instance in which pre-investigation collection of a Schedule B did anything to advance the Attorney General's investigative, regulatory or enforcement efforts."[23]

At the same time, though, the Court expressed great concern that association would be chilled if donors' identity was disclosed. The Court dismissed as irrelevant the fact that California keeps this information secret and that it is the same information that already has to be given to the federal government. Chief Justice Roberts wrote: "Our cases have said that disclosure requirements can chill association '[e]ven if there [is] no disclosure to the general public.'"[24]

The Court thus concluded that the California law was unconstitutional:

> *We are left to conclude that the Attorney General's disclosure requirement imposes a widespread burden on donors' associational rights. And this burden cannot be justified on the ground that the regime is narrowly tailored to investigating charitable wrongdoing, or that the State's interest in administrative convenience is sufficiently important. We therefore hold that the up-front collection of Schedule Bs is facially unconstitutional,*

> *because it fails exacting scrutiny in "a substantial number of its applications . . . judged in relation to [its] plainly legitimate sweep."*[25]

Justice Sotomayor wrote a dissent that was joined by Justices Breyer and Kagan. Justice Sotomayor said that the Court was abandoning its prior decisions which required some proof that association was actually chilled. She wrote:

> *Although this Court is protective of First Amendment rights, it typically requires that plaintiffs demonstrate an actual First Amendment burden before demanding that a law be narrowly tailored to the government's interests, never mind striking the law down in its entirety. Not so today. Today, the Court holds that reporting and disclosure requirements must be narrowly tailored even if a plaintiff demonstrates no burden at all.*[26]

Justice Sotomayor expressed great concern that this will put many other disclosure requirements in jeopardy. She concluded her dissent by saying:

> *Today's decision discards decades of First Amendment jurisprudence recognizing that reporting and disclosure requirements do not directly burden associational rights. There is no other explanation for the Court's conclusion that, first, plaintiffs do not need to show they are actually burdened by a disclosure requirement; second, every disclosure requirement demands narrow tailoring; and third, a facial challenge can succeed in the absence of any evidence a state law burdens the associational rights of a substantial proportion of affected individuals.*[27]

The case raises many questions. What is the difference between "exacting scrutiny" and intermediate scrutiny? Why does the Court use a new level of scrutiny? The classic statement of intermediate scrutiny is that the government action must be substantially related to an important government purpose.[28] As mentioned above, the Court defines exacting scrutiny as requiring "a substantial relation between the disclosure requirement and a sufficiently important governmental interest."[29] The only difference is that intermediate scrutiny says it has to be an "important interest" and exacting scrutiny says it has to be a "sufficiently important interest." But does the word "sufficiently" really add anything? The Court always has to make a judgment of whether a claimed government interest is sufficiently important to meet intermediate scrutiny. It is not clear why the Court makes the choice for exacting scrutiny rather than just using intermediate scrutiny.

Second, what will be the impact on other disclosure requirements? Chief Justice Roberts is explicit that there does not have to be proof that charitable contributions are actually chilled. That is the primary objection in Justice Sotomayor's dissenting opinion. But without requiring some proof it would appear that any disclosure requirement is constitutionally vulnerable. California just was requiring submission to it of a form already being provided to the federal government. Why, then, isn't that federal disclosure requirement also unconstitutional? Will this put campaign disclosure laws in jeopardy?

Third, the Court's decision is based on a concern for chilling association. But the Court in many other cases has been dismissive of claims that government regulation would chill speech. Over a half century ago, in *Younger v. Harris*, the Court declared that "the existence of a 'chilling effect,' even in the area of First Amendment rights, has never been considered a sufficient basis, in and of itself, for prohibiting state action."[30] In *Laird v. Tatum*[31] in 1972 and in *Clapper v. Amnesty International USA*[32] the Court held that a claim that speech was chilled is not a sufficient injury for standing purposes. But in *Americans for Prosperity* the chance of chilling association was enough to violate the First Amendment.

The one thing that can be said for certain about this case is that it is sure to lead to challenges to many other laws requiring disclosure.

Endnotes

1. *See, e.g.*, Citizens United v. Federal Election Commission, 558 U.S. 310 (2010) (declaring unconstitutional restrictions on independent expenditures by corporations).

2. *See* Garcetti v. Ceballos, 547 U.S. 410 (2006).

3. Tinker v. Des Moines Independent Community School District, 393 U.S. 503 (1969).
4. Levy *ex rel.* B.L. v. Mahanoy Area School Dist., 964 F.3d 170 (3d Cir. 2020)
5. 393 U.S. 503 (1969).
6. Id. at 506.
7. Id. at 511.
8. Id. at 505.
9. Bethel School Dist. No. 403 v. Fraser, 478 U.S. 675 (1986).
10. Hazelwood School Dist. v. Kuhlmeier, 484 U.S. 260 (1988).
11. Morse v. Frederick, 551 U.S. 393 (2007).
12. 141 U.S. at 2046.
13. *Id.*
14. *Id.*
15. *Id.* at 2048.
16. *Id.* at 2045.
17. *Id.* at 2059 (Thomas, J., dissenting).
18. Americans for Prosperity Found. v. Bonta, 141 U.S. 2373 (2021).
19. Cal. Govt. Code Ann. § 12584 (West 2018).
20. 141 U.S. at 2391 (Alito, J., concurring in the judgment).
21. *Id.* at 2383.
22. *Id.*
23. *Id.* at 2386.
24. *Id.* at 2388.
25. *Id.* at 2389.
26. *Id.* at 2392 (Sotomayor, J., dissenting).
27. *Bonta*, 141 at 2404.
28. *See* Craig v. Boren, 429 U.S. 190 (1976).
29. *Id.* at 2383.
30. Younger v. Harris, 401 U.S. 37, 51 (1971).
31. Laird v. Tatum, 408 U.S. 1 (1972).
32. Clapper v. Amnesty Int'l USA, 568 U.S. 398 (2013).

9

Immigration Law

Every year the Supreme Court decides a number of cases concerning immigration law and October Term 2020 was no exception. Overall, the Court has taken an approach to interpreting federal immigration statutes that favors the government over claims of non-citizens. Here, too, October Term 2020 was no exception. There were five immigration law decisions and four ruled in favor of the United States.

Pereida v. Wilkinson[1]

Clemente Avelino Pereida is a husband and father of three who came to the United States from Mexico in 1995. He is a Mexican citizen and does not have United States citizenship. Despite this, he had been working in construction and cleaning services, raising his children, and paying taxes to the United States while living here. On August 3, 2009, the Department of Homeland Security (DHS) issued a Notice to Appear (NTA) to Pereida, charging him with "removability." Removability is the process of forcing someone out of the United States, presumably back to the country where the person is a citizen. Pereida conceded that he had never been authorized for a permanent stay in the United States. The circumstances, however, did not permit DHS to automatically deport Pereida, and he applied to have his removal cancelled in March 2011 as is his right under 8 U.S.C. § 1229a(c)(4) of the Immigration and Nationality Act (INA).

In 2014, three years after he applied for cancellation of removal, DHS filed a Motion to Pretermit Pereida's application because in 2010 Nebraska had charged Pereida with using a fraudulent Social Security card in order to obtain employment.[2] He pleaded *nolo contendere* to that offense, accepting the conviction offered but not admitting guilt.

Under 8 U.S.C. § 1229b(1)(c), the Attorney General may cancel the removal of a nonpermanent resident if they have not been convicted of a "crime involving moral turpitude." That phrase, though, is not defined in the law. In Pereida's case, the immigration judge found that a crime involving fraud was, by definition, a crime involving moral turpitude.[3] The Eighth Circuit ruled against Pereida and held that he had the burden of proving that the crime did not involve moral turpitude and that he failed to do so.

The Supreme Court agreed with the Eighth Circuit that Pereida had not met his burden of proof and affirmed the decision to deny his application for removal cancellation in 2021, almost 10 years after he had initially filed it. The majority opinion was written by Justice Gorsuch and joined by Justices Roberts, Thomas, Alito and Kavanaugh. Justice Barrett took no part in the decision.

Gorsuch concluded that Pereida had the burden of proving his crime was not one the court deemed as having moral turpitude. Pereida argued that the court should take a categorical approach in determining the nature of his conviction because the Nebraska statute "criminalizes at least some conduct . . . that doesn't involve fraud" which would mean that violating the statute would not qualify as a crime involving moral turpitude.[4] The Court said that a categorical approach does not adequately inquire into specific facts of the crime committed and that the vagueness of the statutory language requires an in-depth look into the nature of the crime. In other words, whether a crime involves moral turpitude is to be decided based on the acts involved, not how a state defines the offense. The burden of proof has essentially been shifted to defendants, as seen in Pereida's case where Nebraska's vague sentencing and minimal recordkeeping disqualified him from cancelling his removal from the United States.

The dissenting opinion, written by Justice Breyer and joined in by Justices Kagan and Sotomayor, argued that crimes given the label of moral turpitude be treated under a "categorical approach."[5] The approach analyzes whether the crime a person is convicted of is of "moral turpitude" under the language found in state and federal statutes. The dissent said that its approach is preferable because it prevents the Attorney General from "simply deny[ing] relief" when they believe a crime is of moral turpitude without statutory language to back up their belief.[6] In Pereida's case, the state of Nebraska did not specify which of the provisions it accused him of violating. In his case both the majority and the Government "concede[d] that some of the provisions set forth crimes that are not crimes involving moral turpitude."[7] The dissent lamented the broad discretion the decision awards to immigration judges:

> *A noncitizen may agree to plead guilty to a specific offense in a divisible statute because that offense does not carry adverse immigration consequences. But in many lower criminal courts, misdemeanor convictions are not on the record. In jurisdictions where misdemeanor convictions are on the record, such records frequently omit key information about the plea and may be destroyed after only a few years. And even where complete records do exist, noncitizens, who often are unrepresented, detained, or not fluent English speakers, may not have the resources to offer more than their own testimony. Thus, under the majority's approach, noncitizens may lose the benefit of their plea agreements unless their testimony persuades the immigration judge that they pleaded guilty to the lesser offense.*[8]

Niz-Chavez v.Garland[9]

Agusto Niz-Chavez relocated to the United States in 2005 after his family had been forced to leave their land in Guatemala by people of a neighboring village. Niz-Chavez testified that he could not return to his home country because the people who stole his land had threatened to kill him if they discovered he was in Guatemala. He said that the threat needed to be taken seriously as they had killed his brother-in-law. He argued that the people who murdered his family member and stole his family's land have faced no consequences and still reside on the land they stole. In order to protect himself, he applied to cancel his removal in June of 2013. He applied under the language of the Illegal Immigration Reform and Immigrant Responsibility Act of 1996 and also requested relief under the Convention Against Torture.

The United States Court of Appeals for the Sixth Circuit ruled against him, claiming he did not have enough evidence to establish either claim. The Supreme Court focused only on Niz-Chavez's first argument under federal immigration law. The issue involved the statutory requirement found in 8 U.S.C. § 1229b(b)(1) that stated in order to gain relief a person must be "continuously present in the country for at least 10 years."

Although Niz-Chavez had been physically living in the United States for a continuous 10 years as of 2015, the government argued that he was served a Notice to Appear in 2013 by the Department of Homeland Security (DHS) which triggered Congress's "stop time" rule.[10] The statute states that "any period of continuous . . . presence in the United States shall be deemed to end . . . when the alien is served a notice to appear."[11] If the notice by DHS applied, Niz-Chavez would be classified as only living in the U.S. for 8 years and thus ineligible for cancellation of removal. The term "notice to appear" has been interpreted by government officials broadly. DHS does not follow a precise format for the information included in the notices sent and the government claims that any paperwork from DHS labeled as a notice to appear to a noncitizen is adequate to trigger the "stop time" rule.

The Supreme Court disagreed with the government. Justice Gorsuch wrote the opinion for the Court, joined by Justices Thomas, Breyer, Sotomayor, Kagan and Barrett. The Court focused on the language of the statute, which defines a notice to appear as a document which specifies "the nature of the proceedings against the alien, the legal authority for the proceedings, the charges against the alien, the fact that the alien may be represented by counsel, the time and place at which the proceedings will be held, and the consequences of failing to appear."[12]

In Niz-Chavez's case, he was first sent a letter which listed his charges. Two months later he was sent a letter with the time and place of his hearing. The Court concluded that neither of these documents were sufficient to trigger the "stop time" rule. Justice Gorsuch wrote that the key was a single word: "a."[13] He said that by using the indefinite article "a" in front of "notice" Congress indicated that it wanted the notice to be a "discrete, countable thing."[14] The Court said that this was an explicit choice by Congress and shows that they did not intend for the government to treat the notice flexibly. The Court was emphatic that "[a]s written, though, the statute allows the government to invoke the stop-time rule only if it furnishes the alien with a single compliant document explaining what it intends to do and when."[15]

The dissent was written by Justice Kavanaugh and was joined by Chief Justice Roberts and Justice Alito. Kavanaugh argued that the article "a" in "a notice to appear" was not as dispositive as the majority found it to be because the statute never explicitly stated that it required one written notice.[16] The dissent argued that "a" and "one" are different and Congress would have specified "one" had that been its intention. There was concern over how the ruling would affect immigration services, as the majority ruling requires all information to be contained in one document. The dissent contended that Niz-Chavez should have been considered ineligible for cancellation of removal because he was only in the country for 8 consecutive years.

The Roberts Court often stresses following the plain language of the statute in interpreting laws. But this is likely the first case to turn on the meaning of the word "a."

Garland v. Ming Dai[17]

How should issues of fact that turn on credibility be treated in immigration proceedings? Ming Dai and Cesar Alcaraz-Enriquez were each fighting against their deportation charges. In both of their cases, the immigration court found that Dai and Alcaraz-Enriquez had not met the standards necessary to avoid deportation under the Immigration and Nationality Act.

The dispute centered on a difference in the facts reported by the Board of Immigration Appeals (BIA) and the testimonies from each defendant. In both cases, the defendant's testimony presented a different story than the facts provided by the BIA. Alcaraz-Enriquez testified that he had assaulted his girlfriend in protection of his daughter. The Immigration Judge did not consider Alcaraz-Enriquez's story as factual because "there was 'no mention' in the contemporaneous probation report of the girlfriend hitting Mr. Alcaraz-Enriquez's daughter."[18] The lower court found the evidence provided by the BIA to be more compelling than the testimony. The Ninth Circuit reversed by holding that "[w]here the BIA does not make an explicit adverse credibility finding, [the court] must assume that [the alien's] factual contentions are true."[19] Since there was no evidence of the girlfriend not hitting Alcaraz-Enriquez's daughter, then the testimony must be considered true under the Ninth Circuit's precedents.

Dai sought asylum in the U.S and testified that Chinese officials forced his wife to get an abortion and assaulted him when he tried to protect her. He also said that he lost his job, his wife was demoted, and his daughter was denied admission to superior schools after the incident.[20] The BIA found this unconvincing, however, when they discovered that his wife and daughter had voluntarily returned to China. Their return undercut his claim that they would be in danger if they went back and the BIA ruled against him. The Ninth Circuit reversed, saying that there was no evidence to refute his testimony and thus it should be regarded as true.

The Supreme Court unanimously reversed. Justice Gorsuch wrote for the Court and concluded that the Ninth Circuit's approach was not in line with the requirements of the Immigration and Naturalization Act. The Court said that the law "provides that a reviewing court must accept "administrative findings" as "conclusive unless any reasonable adjudicator would be compelled to conclude to the contrary."[21] Justice Gorsuch said that the Ninth Circuit's approach "cannot be reconciled with the INA's terms."[22] The decisions in favor of Dai and Alcaraz-Enriquez were overturned and the cases were remanded.

The unanimous majority opinion states that going forward, immigration cases should proceed by

> *[f]irst, the factfinder—here the IJ—makes findings of fact, including determinations as to the credibility of particular witness testimony. The BIA then reviews those findings, applying a presumption of credibility if the IJ did not make an explicit adverse credibility determination. Finally, the court of appeals*

> *must accept the agency's findings of fact as "conclusive unless any reasonable adjudicator would be compelled to conclude to the contrary.*[23]

This is obviously a much more favorable approach for the government than the Ninth Circuit's handling of factual disputes between immigration authorities and a person facing deportation. No longer is there any presumption of credibility for the unrefuted statements of those facing deportation.

United States v. Palomar-Santiago[24]

Refugio Palomar-Santiago obtained permanent resident status in 1990. In 1991, he was convicted of a felony DUI in California state court. In 1998, he received a Notice to Appear stating that he was subject to removal from the U.S. because his DUI offense was a violent crime and thus an aggravated felony. Palomar-Santiago waived his right to appeal and was removed to Mexico soon after.

In 2017, he was indicted by a grand jury for unlawful reentry after removal. He challenged the indictment under *Leocal v. Ashcroft*,[25] a 2004 decision which reclassified the DUI Palomar-Santiago was convicted of as a non-violent crime and thus not an aggravated felony. He argued that his prior removal was invalid and that he was "excused from proving the first two requirements of § 1326(d)" because he was no longer convicted of an offense that made him removable. The Ninth Circuit ruled in his favor, relying on its earlier decision in *United States v. Ochoa*.[26]

The Supreme Court disagreed and unanimously reversed. Justice Sotomayor wrote for the Court and said that *Ochoa*, and the ruling in Palomar-Santiago's favor, were overruled because they are "incompatible with the text of section 1326(d)."[27] Justice Sotomayor writes "[t]hat section provides that defendants charged with unlawful reentry "may not" challenge their underlying removal orders "unless" they "demonstrat[e]" that three conditions are met: (1) they have "exhausted any administrative remedies," (2) they were "deprived . . . of the opportunity for judicial review," and (3) "the entry of the order was fundamentally unfair."[28] The conjunctive "and" requires that all three conditions must be met, which cannot be reconciled with the Ninth Circuit's reasoning in *Ochoa*. The Court concluded that "each of the statutory requirements of § 1326(d) is mandatory."[29]

Justice Sotomayor explained that the "first two procedural requirements are not satisfied just because a noncitizen was removed for an offense that did not in fact render him removable. Indeed, the substantive validity of the removal order is quite distinct from whether the noncitizen exhausted his administrative remedies (by appealing the immigration judge's decision to the BIA) or was deprived of the opportunity for judicial review (by filing a petition for review of a BIA decision with a Federal Court of Appeals)."[30]

There is an obvious harshness to Palomar-Santiago having been removed from the country for a crime that was later deemed to not be a basis for such removal, and now facing criminal charges for reentry after that wrongful removal. But the Court unanimously said that did not excuse failure to comply with the procedural requirements mandated in the statute.

Sanchez v. Mayorkas[31]

Jose Santos Sanchez is a citizen of El Salvador. Although he was found to have entered the United States illegally in 1997, in 2001 the government granted him Temporary Protection Status (TPS) which allowed him to remain in the United States. Sanchez came to the United States after a series of earthquakes devastated his home. Under immigration law, citizens of certain countries are allowed to obtain Temporary Protection Status despite arriving illegally. Temporary Protected Status entitled him to stay and work in the United States for as long as those conditions persisted.[32]

Sanchez applied to become a lawful permanent resident in 2014. He believed that his nonimmigrant status, which was the result of his Temporary Protection Status, made him eligible for becoming a lawful permanent resident. The issue was whether the conferral of Temporary Protection Status enabled him to obtain lawful permanent resident status despite his unlawful entry.

The Supreme Court unanimously ruled that it does not. Justice Kagan wrote for the Court and said: "TPS program gives foreign nationals nonimmigrant status, but it does not admit them."[33] Lawful Permanent Resident status requires applicants to have been "lawfully admitted" to the United States. The statute does not create an exception for those with Temporary Protection Status.

Justice Kagan concluded by pointing out that Congress could add a lawful admission status for Temporary Protection Status recipients, and that there is indeed current legislation pending in Congress which would do so.[34] But until then, the Court concluded: "Section 1255 generally requires a lawful admission before a person can obtain LPR status. Sanchez was not lawfully admitted, and his TPS does not alter that fact. He therefore cannot become a permanent resident of this country."[35]

Conclusion

None of these cases brought about a major change in immigration law. The inescapable conclusion from these five cases, four of which were won by the government, is that generally the Supreme Court interprets federal immigration law more favorably for the United States government than for non-citizens seeking to remain in the country.

Endnotes

1. Pereida v. Wilkinson, 141 U.S. 754 (2021).
2. Neb. Rev. Stat. Ann. § 28-638 (West 2021).
3. *Pereida, supra* note 1, at 761.
4. *Id.* at 762.
5. *Id.* at 767 (Breyer, J., dissenting).
6. *Id.* at 771.
7. *Id.* at 772.
8. *Id.* at 775.
9. Niz-Chavez v. Barr, 141 U.S. 1474 (2021).
10. *Id.* at 1479.
11. *Id.* (quoting 8 U.S.C.A § 1229b(d)(1) (2021)).
12. *Id.* at 1479.
13. *Id.* at 1486.
14. *Id.*
15. *Id.*

16. *Id.* at 1490 (Kavanaugh, J., dissenting).
17. Garland v. Ming Dai, 141 U.S. 1669 (2021).
18. *Id.* at 1675.
19. *Id.*
20. *Id.* at 1676.
21. *Id.* at 1677.
22. *Id.* at 1681.
23. *Id.*
24. United States v. Palomar-Santiago, 141 U.S. 1615 (2021)
25. Leocal v. Ashcroft 543 U.S. 1, 11-13 (2004)
26. United States v. Ochoa, 861 F.3d 1010 (9th Cir. 2017).
27. *Palomar-Santiago*, *supra* note 24, at 1620.
28. *Id.* at 1620–21 quoting 8 U.S.C. § 1326(d).
29. *Id.* at 1622.
30. *Id.* at 1621.
31. Sanchez v. Mayorkas, 141 S. Ct. 1809 (2021).
32. *See* 8 C.F.R. § 244.3.
33. *Sanchez*, *supra* note 31, at 1812.
34. *See* American Dream and Promise Act of 2021, H. R. 6, 117th Cong., 1st Sess., § 203, p. 29 (introduced Mar. 3, 2021) (amending § 1254a(f)(4)).
35. *Sanchez*, *supra* note 31, at 1815.

10

Indian Law

There were two major decisions concerning Indian Law in October Term 2020. Neither is a major change in the law, but both resolve important issues. One concerns the authority of tribal police to enforce laws on public highways. The other involves the status of Alaska Native Corporations under federal law.

United States v. Cooley[1]

Joshua James Cooley (defendant) was parked on the side of Highway 212, "a public right-of-way within the Crow Reservation, located within the State of Montana."[2] Crow Police Department Officer James Saylor noticed Cooley's truck and approached it, "[b]elieving the occupants might need assistance."[3] When Officer Saylor looked inside, he noticed that Cooley had watery, bloodshot eyes and two semi-automatic rifles on the front seat. He ordered Cooley out of the truck and called tribal and county officers for backup. Saylor then noticed a glass pipe and plastic bag containing methamphetamine. When the other officers arrived, including an officer from the Federal Bureau of Indian Affairs, they instructed Saylor to "seize all contraband in plain view," including the items on the front seat as well as more concealed methamphetamine that was found.[4]

In April 2016, a federal grand jury indicted Cooley on federal drug and gun offenses. The district court granted Cooley's motion to suppress the drug evidence that had been seized because Saylor, as a Crow Tribe police officer, lacked the authority to investigate non-apparent violations of state or federal law by a non-Indian on a public right-of-way crossing the reservation. Saylor never inquired as to whether Cooley was a citizen of the Crow Reservation. Rather, he felt Cooley "appeared to be non-native."[5] Cooley's identity became the main element of the suit. The issue in *United States v. Cooley* was whether a tribal police officer has the authority to temporarily detain and search non-Indians traveling on public right-of-ways running through a reservation for potential violations of state or federal law. The District Court and the Ninth Circuit both held that tribal officers lacked that authority, meaning Cooley had been detained and searched unlawfully.

But the Supreme Court disagreed and reversed. Justice Breyer, writing for a unanimous Court, began by citing to the key precedent: *Montana v. United States*.[6] In *Montana*, the Court held that the Crow Tribe could not regulate hunting and fishing by non-Indians on their reservation on land that non-members of the tribe owned in fee simple. The Court had previously opined that "a tribe could not exercise criminal jurisdiction over non-Indians."[7] However, the *Montana* Court qualified its central holding with two important exceptions: (1) a tribe may regulate, through taxation, licensing, or other means, the activities of nonmembers who enter consensual relationships with the tribe or its members, through commercial dealing, contracts, leases, or other arrangements, and (2) a tribe may also retain inherent power to exercise civil authority over the conduct of non-Indians on fee lands within its reservation when that conduct threatens or has some direct effect on the political integrity, the economic security, or the health or welfare of the tribe.

The Supreme Court said that the facts of *Cooley* fit the second exception "like a glove."[8] Justice Breyer clarified that Cooley was not subject to tribal laws. Rather, only "state and federal laws that apply whether an individual is outside a reservation or on a state or federal highway within it."[9] Justice Breyer reasoned that tribal jurisdiction would have been denied if Saylor had detained Cooley under Crow Tribe specific laws. But here, Cooley had been detained and searched for a suspected violation of federal drug and gun laws, not tribal law.

Cooley argued that the tribal officers should be required to verify that anyone they anticipate they will detain be identified as either Indian or non-Indian. But the Court disagreed with Cooley. Such a stringent requirement would be logistically challenging for tribal officers. Furthermore, the public interest in safety outweighs the need to differentiate between tribal members and non-tribal members. Ultimately, the Court found that tribal officers have the right to detain and search whoever is on tribal land, so long as they do not subject that person to non-federal or non-state laws. Cooley's detention and search by tribal officers, performed in enforcement of federal criminal law, was constitutional.

Justice Alito wrote a short concurrence to clarify his understanding of the holding. He perceives it as:

> *[N]o more than the following: On a public right-of-way that traverses an Indian reservation and is primarily patrolled by tribal police, a tribal police officer has the authority to (a) stop a non-Indian motorist if the officer has reasonable suspicion that the motorist may violate or has violated federal or state law, (b) conduct a search to the extent necessary to protect himself or others, and (c) if the tribal officer has probable cause, detain the motorist for the period of time reasonably necessary for a non-tribal officer to arrive on the scene.*[10]

The *Cooley* decision will be celebrated as a win for tribal sovereignty and the ability of tribal police to enforce the law within their territories. But the actual ruling in this case is narrow in scope; it is limited to the power of tribe police to enforce federal and state law on public highways. Also, the Court emphasized that "in all cases, tribal authority remains subject to the plenary authority of Congress."[11]

Yellen v. Confederated Tribes of the Chehalis Reservation[12]

In *Yellen v. Confederated Tribes of the Chehalis Reservation*, the Supreme Court considered the issue of whether Alaska Native Corporations (ANC) are "Indian Tribes" under the Indian Self-Determination and Education

Assistance Act (ISDA) and therefore qualified for money from the Coronavirus Aid, Relief, and Economic Security Act (CARES). This is not the first time the Supreme Court has ruled on whether Alaska Native Corporations fit within the "Indian Tribe" label of ISDA. The relationship between Alaskan Natives and the United States government is distinct from federally recognized tribes. Alaskan Native people are distinguished from Native Americans in the lower 48 states because they were not forced into official reservations by the American government until the 1970s. The Alaska Native Claims Settlement Act (ANCSA) extinguished Alaska Natives' claims to land and hunting rights and revoked all but one of Alaska's existing reservations. In exchange, Congress authorized the transfer of $962.5 million in state and federal funds and approximately 44 million acres of Alaska land to state-chartered private business corporations that were to be formed pursuant to ANCSA.

The Secretary of the Interior divided Alaska into 12 geographic regions and forced Alaska Natives to incorporate under the laws of Alaska Regional Corporations to conduct business for profit. The ANCs were established wherever the 1970 U.S. census found that 25 or more Alaska Natives lived together. The "ANCSA ordered the 'Native residents' to create an accompanying village corporation to 'hold, invest, manage and/or distribute lands, property, funds, and other rights and assets for and on behalf of the village.'"[13] The Secretary of the Interior created a list of the regions and villages where every Native Alaskan person lived. Enrolled Alaskan Natives then received shares in their respective ANCs.

The Indian Self-Determination and Education Assistance Act was passed in 1975, four years after the Alaska Native Claims Settlement Act was enacted. ISDA allows for Indian Tribes to contract with the Secretary of the Interior to deliver "federally funded economic, infrastructure, health, or education benefits to the tribe's membership."[14] ISDA explicitly included ANCs within its definition of Indian Tribes.

The Ute Indian Tribe of the Uintah and Ouray Reservation argued that ANCs were barred from CARES Act relief because the CARES Act restricted allocated money to "tribal governments" and ANCs have no recognized governing body that would qualify them as tribal governments under the Act. The challengers also claimed that ANCs cannot be considered federally recognized tribes because there is no government-to-government relationship between ANCs and the United States government. Thus, the challengers conclude that ANCs do not qualify for CARES Act funding.

The Supreme Court, however, rejected the tribe's argument in a 6–3 decision. Justice Sotomayor wrote the opinion, which was joined in full by Justices Breyer, Kavanaugh, Barrett and Chief Justice Roberts, and joined in part by Justice Alito. The *Yellen* Court began by referencing the provision of the CARES Act that defines "tribal government" as what its definition is under the ISDA. The ISDA lists ANCs as tribal governments. So, the Court concluded that Congress's definition of tribal government under the CARES Act included ANCs. Rebutting the challenger's claim about a lack of government-to-government relationship, the Court said that the ISDA applies the "recognized governing body" standard to an ANCs board of directors. The Court stated:

> *If Congress did not want to make ANCs eligible for CARES Act funding, its decision to incorporate ISDA's "Indian tribe" definition into the CARES Act would be inexplicable. Had Congress wished to limit CARES Act funding to federally recognized tribes, it could simply have cross-referenced the List Act instead, as it had in numerous statutes before.*[15]

The majority opinion was clear that *any* legislation which refers to ISDA's definition of Indian Tribes includes ANCs.

The dissent was authored by Justice Gorsuch and joined by Justices Thomas and Kagan. Gorsuch's dissent argued that ANCs do *not* qualify as tribal governments as defined by the CARES Act. Justice Gorsuch reached this conclusion by examining the grammatical structure of the ISDA and how the law spoke of "Indian tribe[s], band[s], nation[s]."[16] Justice Gorsuch argued that Congress sought to encourage tribal self-governance with the passage of ISDA. Therefore, only government-to-government relationships between tribes and the U.S. government meet the ISDA standard. As entities lacking that relationship with the U.S. government, ANCs were excluded from the CARES Act. Gorsuch wrote:

> *[O]ur disagreement is simply about applying the plain meaning, grammar, context, and canons of construction to the particular*

> *statutory terms before us. As I see it, an ordinary reader would understand that the recognition clause applies the same way to all Indian groups. And if that's true, there's just no way to read the text to include ANCs as 'Tribal governments' for purposes of the CARES Act.*[17]

The *Yellen* decision is important in that it holds that Alaska Native Corporations are to be regarded as Native American tribes for purposes of federal law. Most significantly of all, it means that ANCs can receive substantial funds under the CARES Act.

Endnotes

1. 141 S. Ct. 1638 (2021).
2. *Id.* at 1642.
3. *Id.*
4. *Id.*
5. *Id.*
6. 450 U.S. 544 (1981).
7. 141 S. Ct. at 1643 (quotations omitted).
8. *Id.*
9. *Id.* at 1645.
10. *Id.* at 1646 (Alito, J., concurring).
11. *Id.* at 1643.
12. 141 S. Ct. 2434 (2021).
13. *Id.* at 2439.
14. *Id.*
15. *Id.* at 2451.
16. *Id.* at 2453 (Gorsuch, J., dissenting) (quoting another source).
17. *Id.* at 2460 (Gorsuch, J., dissenting).

11

Intellectual Property

For those who practice in the field of intellectual property law, no case was more important this term than *Google LLC v. Oracle America, Inc.*[1] It is one of the most important copyright cases, if not *the* most significant, in the internet era.

Facts

Sun Microsystems developed the Java programming language. When Google acquired Android and decided to move into the mobile phone business, they wanted to use Java SE to create the operating system (OS) for their mobile devices. Android is now the most widely used operating system on mobile devices in the world, used on over 2.5 billion active devices produced by more than 180 hardware manufacturers.[2] Using Java, a familiar and widely known language to many programmers, would facilitate interoperability among devices and between programs because software developers were already familiar with the language. Developers who were familiar with the coding language could more easily develop programs that would work with Google's new operating system.

After negotiations to obtain a license to use Java deteriorated, Google copied 11,500 lines of code from the Java SE platform which constituted

0.4% of the entire platform. With the exception of a few programs not at issue before the Supreme Court, Google copied only Java's "declaring code," not its "implementing code." In other words, Google copied the names of Java SE's mini-programs but re-wrote the programs themselves. These lines executed many common functions in Java and allowed a programmer to call up prewritten functions without having to re-write each function each time they wanted to import that function into other coding lines. This simplified the code itself and made it much easier for developers to work with the new Android OS. It's similar to being able to use the command function "underline" to underline a phrase in a Word document, rather than having to use words to define what "underline" means. Justice Breyer explained the importance of this:

> *The copied lines of code are part of a tool called an Application Programming Interface, or API. What is an API? The Federal Circuit described an API as a tool that 'allow[s] programmers to use . . . prewritten code to build certain functions into their own programs, rather than write their own code to perform those functions from scratch.' Through an API, a programmer can draw upon a vast library of prewritten code to carry out complex tasks. . . .*
>
> *Consider in more detail just what an API does. A computer can perform thousands, perhaps millions, of different tasks that a programmer may wish to use. These tasks range from the most basic to the enormously complex. Ask the computer, for example, to tell you which of two numbers is the higher number or to sort one thousand numbers in ascending order, and it will instantly give you the right answer.*[3]

Oracle acquired Sun Microsystems and sued Google for copyright infringement. The litigation has a long history. After a jury trial, the United States District Court for the Northern District of California entered judgment in favor of Google on patent claims and entered judgment in favor of Oracle in part and for Google in part on copyright claims. The court concluded that the declaring code's "structure, sequence, and organization" was not eligible for copyright protection because it was a "method of operation." The Federal Circuit reversed, holding that the copied lines are copyrightable. Subsequently, a jury found that Google's copying was fair use and could not be the basis for liability for copyright infringement.

The Federal Circuit reversed once more, concluding that Google's copying was not fair use. Prior to remand for a trial on damages, the Supreme Court agreed to review the Federal Circuit's determination as to both copyrightability and fair use.

The Court's Decision

There were two issues before the Supreme Court: First, is Java's API copyrightable? This involved how to resolve tension between two of the statutory provisions in the copyright law, one that permits copyrighting computer programs and the other that provides that copyright will not subsist in "process[es]," "system[s]," and "method[s] of operation." The Supreme Court chose not to answer this question, but instead to assume copyrightability. Justice Breyer, writing for the majority, said: "We shall assume, but purely for argument's sake, that the entire Sun Java API falls within the definition of that which can be copyrighted."[4]

The Court thus focused exclusively on the second issue: was Google's action fair use under the Copyright Act? The Court said yes, with Justices Thomas and Alito dissenting.

At the outset, the Court held that fair use is a mixed question of law and fact. The facts are decided by a jury, but a judge must decide if the facts constitute fair use. Courts should defer to the jury's finding of facts, but the ultimate question of whether those facts amount to fair use is a legal question for judges. This approach does not violate the Seventh Amendment's constraints of the ability of judges to reexamine facts decided by a jury because the ultimate question is one of law. The Court declared: "the ultimate question whether those facts showed a 'fair use' is a legal question for judges to decide *de novo*."[5]

Section 107 of the Copyright Act identifies four non-exclusive factors to be considered in determining whether there is fair use:

> (1) the purpose and character of the use, including whether such use is of a commercial nature or is for nonprofit educational purposes;
>
> (2) the nature of the copyrighted work;
>
> (3) the amount and substantiality of the portion used in relation to the copyrighted work as a whole; and
>
> (4) the effect of the use upon the potential market for or value of the copyrighted work.

The Court held that the first factor weighed in favor of Google. Justice Breyer characterized Android as "a highly creative and innovative tool . . . consistent with the creative 'progress' that is the basic constitutional objective of copyright itself."[6] To the majority, this indicated that "Google's copying was transformative."[7] Transformativeness is an important, and sometimes dispositive, element of the fair use analysis. A work is transformative if "the copier's use 'adds something new, with a further purpose or different character, altering' the copyrighted work 'with new expression, meaning or message.'"[8]

Google's limited copying of the API was deemed transformative use because Google's purpose was to create a different system for a different computing environment, mobile devices, and to develop the Android platform that would help achieve that purpose. The Court noted that the record demonstrates many ways in which reimplementing an interface can further the development of computer programs. The Court concluded: "These and related facts convince us that the 'purpose and character' of Google's copying was transformative—to the point where this factor too weighs in favor of fair use."[9]

As for the second factor, Justice Breyer said that the computer program here is further from the core of what copyright law seeks to protect. He explained:

Like other computer programs, it is functional in nature. But unlike many other programs, its use is inherently bound together with uncopyrightable ideas (general task division and organization) and new creative expression (Android's implementing code). Unlike many other programs, its value in significant part derives from the value that those who do not hold copyrights, namely, computer programmers, invest of their own time and effort to learn the API's system. And unlike many other programs, its value lies in its efforts to encourage programmers to learn and to use that system so that they will use (and continue to use) Sun-related implementing programs that Google did not copy.[10]

The Court held "the declaring code is, if copyrightable at all, further than most computer programs (such as implementing code) from the core of copyright."[11] The second fair use factor thus tipped in favor of Google and a finding of fair use.

As for the third factor—the amount and substantiality of the use—the Court observed that Google copied 11,500 lines of code from the API, which is all the "declaring code" needed to call up hundreds of different tasks. However, the 11,500 lines are only 0.4% of the entire 2.86 million lines of code in the API. The Federal Circuit had held below that only 170 lines of code are "necessary to write in the Java language." The Court stressed that "[i]n our view, that conclusion views Google's legitimate objectives too narrowly. Google's basic objective was not simply to make the Java programming language usable on its Android systems. It was to permit programmers to make use of their knowledge and experience using the Sun Java API when they wrote new programs for smartphones with the Android platform."[12] Therefore, although Google had taken a significant quantity of code, it did not take more than it needed. The Court held that the third factor weighed in Google's favor.

Crucial for Justice Breyer was the public benefit from Google's use of the Java SE program. He was explicit in stressing the importance of focusing on these benefits in fair use analysis.

Further, we must take into account the public benefits the copying will likely produce. Are those benefits, for example,

> *related to copyright's concern for the creative production of new expression? Are they comparatively important, or unimportant, when compared with dollar amounts likely lost (taking into account as well the nature of the source of the loss)?*[13]

The Court said that the fourth statutory factor, "the effect" of the copying in the "market for or value of the copyrighted work" also weighs in favor of fair use. The record showed that Google's Android platform is not a market substitute for Java SE. Moreover, the record demonstrated that Java SE's copyright holder would benefit from its introduction into another market. Enforcing the copyright on these facts risks causing reactivity related harms to the public.

Justice Breyer, writing for the Court, concluded:

> *The fact that computer programs are primarily functional makes it difficult to apply traditional copyright concepts in that technological world. In doing so here, we have not changed the nature of those concepts. . . .*
>
> *We reach the conclusion that in this case, where Google reimplemented a user interface, taking only what was needed to allow users to put their accrued talents to work in a new and transformative program, Google's copying of the Sun Java API was a fair use of that material as a matter of law.*[14]

Justice Thomas wrote a strong dissent, joined by Justice Alito. He criticized the majority for not reaching the issue as to whether this computer code was copyrightable. Justice Thomas thought it clearly should have been deemed to be copyrightable and that the failure of the Court to address this distorted its analysis.

For Justice Thomas there was a fundamental unfairness in Google using the Java program without a license and making a huge profit as a result. By contrast, the majority mostly disregarded bad faith as not necessarily relevant to the fair use inquiry. Justice Thomas began his dissent by noting:

> *Google sought a license to use the library in Android, the operating system it was developing for mobile phones. But when the companies could not agree on terms, Google simply copied verbatim 11,500 lines of code from the library. As a result, it erased 97.5% of the value of Oracle's partnership with Amazon, made tens of billions of dollars, and established its position as the owner of the largest mobile operating system in the world.*[15]

Justice Thomas argued that three of the fair use factors weigh in favor of Oracle and against Google's fair use. He said that the most important element of fair use is Google's effect on the market for the value of Oracle's work and that this strongly favored ruling against Google:

> *Google eliminated the reason manufacturers were willing to pay to install the Java platform. Google's business model differed from Oracle's. While Oracle earned revenue by charging device manufacturers to install the Java platform, Google obtained revenue primarily through ad sales. Its strategy was to release Android to device manufacturers for free and then use Android as a vehicle to collect data on consumers and deliver behavioral ads. With a free product available that included much of Oracle's code (and thus with similar programming potential), device manufacturers no longer saw much reason to pay to embed the Java platform.*
>
> *For example, before Google released Android, Amazon paid for a license to embed the Java platform in Kindle devices. But after Google released Android, Amazon used the cost-free availability of Android to negotiate a 97.5% discount on its license fee with Oracle. Evidence at trial similarly showed that right after Google released Android, Samsung's contract with Oracle dropped from $40 million to about $1 million.*[16]

Justice Thomas made clear that he thought that the majority erred both in not addressing copyrightability and in finding fair use.

Implications

The difference between the majority's reasoning and that of the dissent is instructive. For the majority the key holding is that Google's use was transformative and that there was a strong public benefit which outweighed any harms to Oracle. Indeed, Justice Breyer's opinion says relatively little about the economic harms to Oracle from Google's copying of the computer code from the Java SE program. By contrast, Justice Thomas, in dissent, focuses on the harm to Oracle as a primary consideration and gives relatively little weight to the transformative use of the program or the public benefit resulting from it.

For copyright cases in the future, the majority's approach to fair use is likely to be very important in its emphasis on whether the use is transformative and the public benefit. And, of course, the Court leaves open whether such computer code is copyrightable at all.

Endnotes

1. 141 S. Ct. 1183 (2021).
2. Taylor Kerns, *There are now more than 2.5 billion active Android devices, Android Police*, May 7, 2019 https://www.androidpolice.com/2019/05/07/there-are-now-more-than-2-5-billion-active-android-devices/.
3. *Id.* at 1191.
4. *Id.* at 1196.
5. *Id.* at 1199.
6. *Id.* at 1203.
7. *Id.* at 1204.
8. *Id.* at 1203.
9. *Id.* at 1204.
10. *Id.* at 1202.
11. *Id.*
12. *Id.* at 1205.
13. *Id.* at 1206.
14. *Id.* 1208–09.
15. *Id.* at 1210–11 (Thomas, J., dissenting).
16. *Id.* at 1216.

12

Personal Jurisdiction

For the last two decades, the Supreme Court has consistently restricted the ability to sue out-of-state defendants without their consent. But in *Ford Motor Company v. Montana Eighth Judicial District*, the Court allowed an out-of-state company to be sued.[1] The decision is important for clarifying the law of personal jurisdiction, but it also raises many questions which will confront lower state and federal courts and ultimately need Supreme Court resolution.

Background

Every first-year law student in Civil Procedure reads the famous case of *International Shoe v. State of Washington*.[2] Even before this case, the Court long had ruled that due process limits the ability to sue an out-of-state defendant without their consent.[3] In *International Shoe*, the Supreme Court held that unless the defendant consents to jurisdiction of the court, an out-of-state defendant can be sued only if it has "minimum contacts" with a state. The Court found that the activities of the sales personnel of an out-of-state shoe company—exhibiting samples of merchandise and soliciting orders from prospective buyers—were systematic and continuous and carried out to result in a large volume of interstate business. The Court thus found personal jurisdiction over the shoe company. The opinion reasoned that that it is constitutionally permissible to sue out of state defendants when they have minimum contacts with the state where a lawsuit is brought. These continuous and systematic minimum contacts alleviate the risk that "notions of fair play and substantial justice" would be offended by finding personal jurisdiction over an out of state defendant

In the decades after *International Shoe*, the Court found two ways of finding minimum contacts: general jurisdiction and specific jurisdiction. Not all Supreme Court decisions about personal jurisdiction used these concepts, but in recent years the Court increasingly has invoked them in analyzing issues of personal jurisdiction. Both general and specific jurisdiction have been greatly narrowed in recent years. It used to be that general jurisdiction could be found if the defendant, in the words of *International Shoe*, had "systematic and continuous contacts" with the state. But in cases such as *Goodyear Dunlop Tires Operations, S. A. v. Brown* (2011)[4] and *Daimler AG v. Bauman* (2014),[5] the Court held that general jurisdiction exists only when a defendant is "essentially at home" in the State. An individual is subject to general jurisdiction in his or her state of domicile, and a corporation is "home" in the state where it is incorporated or has its principal place of business.

Specific jurisdiction exists where the defendant's contacts with the state give rise to the cause of action. In recent years, the Court has restricted this type of jurisdiction too. For example, in *Walden v. Fiore* (2014), the Court stressed that it is not enough that the defendant's conduct would foreseeably cause injury in a state; there is not personal jurisdiction if the defendant did not have the requisite contacts with the state where the suit is brought.[6]

Most recently in *Bristol-Myers Squibb Co.* v. *Superior Court of Cal., San Francisco Cty.*, (2017), the Court refused to allow out-of-state plaintiffs to sue a drug company for harms they suffered.[7] Even though the out of state plaintiffs were part of a lawsuit brought by plaintiffs in their home state, had suffered the same injury as the in-state plaintiffs, and the drug they were suing over was marketed and sold in California, in an 8-1 decision the Court rejected the existence of personal jurisdiction. The Court said that for specific jurisdiction "there must be an affiliation between the forum and the underlying controversy, principally, [an] activity or an occurrence that takes place in the forum State" and is therefore subject to the State's regulation.[8] The Court stressed that personal jurisdiction is not only about fairness to the defendant; it also is about the constitutional limits on the reach of a state's territorial authority.

There is no doubt that this trend in the law greatly favors defendants, making it harder to hale them to other states to be sued, and more difficult for plaintiffs to bring suits in convenient forums. In light of this trend, crucial question is how much further the Court would go in limiting personal jurisdiction.

Suits against Ford Motor Company

Two cases came to the Supreme Court together that involved individuals who had been injured by Ford Motor vehicles. Markkaya Gullett was driving a 1996 Ford Explorer near her home in Montana when the tread separated from a rear tire. The vehicle spun out, rolled, and came to rest upside down. She died in the accident and her estate sued Ford in Montana.

Adam Bandemer was a passenger in his friend's Ford Crown Victoria in Minnesota where he lived. The car was in an accident and Bandemer's air bag failed to deploy. He was severely injured, including suffering serious brain damage. He sued Ford in Minnesota state court.

Ford moved to dismiss both suits for lack of personal jurisdiction. There was no general jurisdiction over Ford because it was not incorporated and did not have its principal place of business in either Montana or Minnesota. Ford argued that there also was not specific jurisdiction because in neither case had its contact with the states given rise to the cause of action there. Ford emphasized that neither vehicle had been sold in the state where the accident occurred. The Explorer was initially sold in Washington and the Crown Victoria in North Dakota. As the Court noted, "[o]nly later resales and relocations by consumers had brought the vehicles to Montana and Minnesota."[9] Ford further argued that specific jurisdiction had not been met because it had designed the Explorer and Crown Victoria in Michigan, and it had manufactured the cars in (respectively) Kentucky and Canada.

Supreme Court Finds Personal Jurisdiction

The Supreme Court ruled against Ford in both cases, issuing a single opinion. The result was unanimous, with Justice Kagan writing for five justices. Justice Alito wrote an opinion concurring in the judgment, as did Justice Gorsuch joined by Justice Thomas. Justice Barrett did not participate because she was not on the bench when the cases were argued in October 2020.

The Court declared: "When a company like Ford serves a market for a product in a State and that product causes injury in the State to one of its residents, the State's courts may entertain the resulting suit."[10] Justice Kagan's majority opinion stressed two factors in finding specific jurisdiction: purposeful availment and relatedness.

As for the former, the Court said that Ford had purposely availed itself of both Montana and Minnesota in its marketing, sales, and serving of cars in those states. The Court noted,

> *By every means imaginable—among them, billboards, TV and radio spots, print ads, and direct mail—Ford urges Montanans and Minnesotans to buy its vehicles, including (at all relevant times) Explorers and Crown Victorias. Ford cars—again including those two models—are available for sale, whether new or used, throughout the States, at 36 dealerships in Montana and 84 in Minnesota.*[11]

As for "relatedness," the Court stressed that "Ford had systematically served a market in Montana and Minnesota for the very vehicles that the plaintiffs allege malfunctioned and injured them in those States. So there is a strong 'relationship among the defendant, the forum, and the litigation'—the 'essential foundation' of specific jurisdiction."[12] The fact that the vehicles were purchased in other states did not matter. The Court explained that Ford's marketing in the states where the suits were brought and the availability of its service there well could have caused these plaintiffs to purchase the Ford vehicles.

Justice Gorsuch wrote a concurring opinion in which he suggested that it might be time to reconsider *International Shoe* and start over in developing the jurisprudence of personal jurisdiction. He said:

> *Maybe, too, International Shoe just doesn't work quite as well as it once did. For a period, its specific jurisdiction test might have seemed a reasonable new substitute for assessing corporate "presence," a way to identify those out-of-state corporations that were simply pretending to be absent from jurisdictions where they were really transacting business. When a company "purposefully availed" itself of the benefits of another State's market in the 1940s, it often involved sending in agents, advertising in local media, or developing a network of on-the-ground dealers, much as Ford did in these cases. But, today, even an individual retiree carving wooden decoys in Maine can "purposefully avail" himself of the chance to do business across the continent after drawing online orders to his e-Bay "store" thanks to Internet advertising with global reach. A test once aimed at keeping corporations honest about their out-of-state operations now seemingly risks hauling individuals to jurisdictions where they have never set foot.*[13]

It is not clear whether Justice Gorsuch is questioning the idea of "minimum contacts," which comes from *International Shoe*, or the subsequent formulations of general and specific jurisdiction. Also, it is not clear what Justice Gorsuch would use instead if minimum contacts is jettisoned as the test for personal jurisdiction. But it is notable that he questions the approach to personal jurisdiction that has been used since 1945 when *International Shoe* was decided.

Questions Left Open

The Court's decision is significant, in part, because for the first time in years, the justices were willing to find personal jurisdiction over an out-of-state defendant. The decision will be important in countless cases for its clarification that specific jurisdiction is to be determined by purposeful availment and relatedness.

But many questions remain. First, how is this case different from *Bristol Myers Squibb v. Superior Court*, decided just four years earlier? That case involved out-of-state plaintiffs (as well as in-state plaintiffs) suing a major corporation that aggressively marketed and sold drugs in the state where it was sued. And the lawsuit was for a particular drug that it regularly sold in that state. In her opinion in *Ford Motor Company v. Montana Eighth Judicial District*, Justice Kagan distinguished the case based on the plaintiffs. She said that in *Bristol Myers Squibb* the out-of-state plaintiffs had not been prescribed the drug, Plavix, in California, and had not ingested it there or been injured there. She said, "[i]n short, the plaintiffs were engaged in forum-shopping—suing in California because it was thought plaintiff-friendly, even though their cases had no tie to the State."[14] But personal jurisdiction always has historically focused on the *defendant's* contacts with the forum state. Indeed, a defendant can consent to personal jurisdiction even if is completely absent in a state. Has the Court now explicitly made the plaintiff's contacts important in personal jurisdiction analysis as well?

Second, what does "serve a market" mean? What does it mean to "cause an injury in the state"? This was an easy case given Ford Motor Company's size and aggressive marketing in these states. But there is going to be much litigation over how to apply the Court's holding to cases that are not as easy, and how these lines are to be drawn.

Third, what will be the importance of the concurring opinions in the judgment, especially Justice Gorsuch's? Justice Gorsuch questions *International Shoe* and especially the distinction between general and specific jurisdiction (which he mistakenly attributes to that decision). Justice Alito, in his opinion, says, "To be sure, for the reasons outlined in Justice Gorsuch's thoughtful opinion, there are grounds for questioning the standard that the Court adopted in *International Shoe Co. v. Washington*."[15] Might this suggest even more major changes in the law of personal jurisdiction in the future?

Endnotes

1. Ford Motor Co. v. Mont. Eighth Jud. Dist., 141 S. Ct. 1017 (2021).
2. Int'l Shoe Co. v. Wash. Off. of Unemp. Comp. and Placement, 326 U.S. 310 (1945).
3. *See* Pennoyer v. Neff, 95 U.S. 714 (1878).

4. Goodyear Dunlop Tires Operations, S. A. v. Brown, 564 U.S. 915, 924 (2011).

5. Daimler AG v. Bauman, 571 U.S. 117, 122 (2014).

6. Walden v. Fiore, 571 U.S. 277, 289–290 (2014).

7. Bristol-Myers Squibb Co. v. Superior Court of Cal., San Francisco Cty., 137 S. Ct. 1773, 1781 (2017).

8. *Id.* at 1780 (quoting *Goodyear Dunlop Tires Operations*, *supra* note 4, at 919).

9. *See Ford Motor Co.*, *supra* note 1, at 1023.

10. *Id.* at 1022.

11. *Id.* at 1028.

12. *Id.*

13. *Id.* at 1038 (Gorsuch, J., concurring).

14. *Id.* at 1031.

15. *Id.* at 1032 (Alito, J., concurring).

13

Separation of Powers

In recent years, the Supreme Court has increasingly adopted the "unitary executive" theory, strengthening the power of the President to appoint and remove executive officials and declaring unconstitutional laws limiting this authority. This is an approach that stresses that the President is in charge of the entire executive branch of government and that invalidates restrictions on his control. There were important cases this term involving both the presidential appointment and removal powers. These cases fit within the striking pattern of recent years in strengthening the President's powers and limiting congressional authority.

Appointment Power

Article II, § 2, provides that the president "shall nominate, and by and with the Advice and Consent of the Senate, shall appoint Ambassadors, other public Ministers and Consuls, Judges of the Supreme Court, and all other Officers of the United States, whose Appointments are not herein otherwise provided for, and which shall be established by Law: but the Congress may by Law vest the Appointment of such inferior Officers, as they think proper, in the President alone, to the Courts of Law, or in the Heads of Departments." In other words, the Constitution says that the

President alone appoints officers of the United States, but it gives some discretion to Congress as to who can appoint inferior officers.

There are relatively few cases defining the line between officers and inferior officers. A recent 2018 case, concerning the definition of "officers" was *Lucia v. Securities and Exchange Commission.*[1] In *Lucia*, the Court considered whether administrative law judges in the Securities and Exchange Commission should be regarded as "Officers of the United States"—rather than mere employees of the federal government—and therefore whether these officers must be appointed by the President, a court of law, or a head of department.

The Securities and Exchange Commission instituted a proceeding against Raymond Lucia for deceiving prospective clients about a retirement savings strategy called "Buckets of Money." The case was adjudicated by an administrative law judge (ALJ), who found Lucia guilty and imposed sanctions, including $300,000 in civil penalties and a lifetime bar from the investment industry.

In his appeal, Lucia argued that the administrative appeal was invalid because the ALJ had not been constitutionally appointed. Lucia argued that ALJs are officers of the United States and subject to the Appointments Clause. He stated that the ALJ had not been appointed by the President, a court of law, or a head of department and therefore their appointment was unconstitutional.

Justice Kagan, writing for the majority, said that under *Freytag v. Commissioner*, ALJs should be considered officers of the United States.[2] In *Freytag*, the Court had held that the special tax judges of the United States Tax Court are officers of the United States. The Court based its holding on the idea that these tax judges held a "continuing office" and exercised "significant discretion."[3]

The Court in *Lucia* concluded that administrative law judges likewise hold continuing offices and exercise significant discretion. Justice Kagan, writing for the Court, explained:

> *Freytag says everything necessary to decide this case. To begin, the Commission's ALJs, like the Tax Court's STJs, hold a continuing office established by law. . . . Far from serving temporarily or episodically, SEC ALJs "receive[ ] a career appointment."*

> *Still more, the Commission's ALJs exercise the same "significant discretion" when carrying out the same 'important functions' as STJs do.*[4]

The Court thus ruled that Lucia should get a new hearing before a properly appointed officer of the United States. This, of course, affects administrative law judges throughout the federal government. The SEC only has five ALJs, but the Social Security Administration has 1,500. It is hard to see how Social Security ALJ's would be any different from the ALJs at the SEC. That means Congress will have to decide whether to have them appointed by the President, the federal courts, or most likely the heads of departments.

But the Court also left open many questions. The Court did not definitively say what would make someone an inferior officer. What authority is enough to make someone an officer of the United States? Also, once they are deemed "officers" what is the constitutionality of limits on removal? The Court did not address this issue, though it was briefed in the case and raised by Justice Breyer.[5]

This term, the Court returned to this issue in two cases. One case followed directly from *Lucia*: *Carr v. Saul*.[6] The six petitioners applied for disability benefits between 2013 and 2015 with the Social Security Administration (SSA) and were denied relief by their respective SSA administrative law judges (ALJ). After *Lucia v. SEC* came down in 2018, petitioners argued that the ALJs who denied their claims were appointed unconstitutionally, as they were appointed by lower-level staff. They argued that this violated the Appointments Clause, which states that "only the President, Courts of Law, or Heads of Departments may appoint Officers of the United States." The Commissioner of the SSA did not dispute that the ALJs who ruled on the cases were unconstitutionally appointed at the time of the decisions, but "contended instead that petitioners had forfeited their Appointments Clause challenges by failing to raise them before the agency."

Justice Sotomayor wrote the opinion on behalf of the entire bench. The unanimous Court found that the petitioners "had exhausted the full set of available administrative review procedures" and thus were correct in asserting their right to bring a constitutional claim despite not raising the challenge in administrative proceedings.[7] However, Justice Sotomayor acknowledged that the "SSA ALJs have no special expertise and . . . can provide no relief" for the challenge brought by the petitioners.[8] The Court ruled that petitioners should be allowed hearings in front of constitutionally appointed ALJ's in light of *Lucia*.

The other and likely more significant case this term was *United States v. Arthrex, Inc.*[9] Arthrex, Inc is a medical equipment manufacturing company which specializes in devices and procedures for orthopedic surgery. In 2015, it secured a patent on a surgical device for reattaching soft tissue to bone without tying a knot. Shortly after, Arthrex claimed that Smith & Nephew and ArthroCare Corp infringed its patent. The dispute reached the Patent Trial and Appeal Board (PTAB) within the Patent and Trademark Office (PTO), and the PTAB "concluded that a prior patent application 'anticipated,' [or had previously described or claimed] the invention claimed by [Anthrex's patent], so that [it] was invalid."[10]

Arthrex fought this decision under the Appointments Clause of the Constitution, arguing that the Administrative Patent Judges (APJ) were unconstitutionally appointed. As explained above, the Appointment Clause distinguishes agency leaders as principal or inferior officers, and "[p]rincipal officers must be appointed by the President with the advice and consent of the Senate, while inferior officers may be appointed by the President alone, the head of an executive department, or a court." APJs are appointed to the PTAB by the Secretary of Commerce, which suggests that they are classified as inferior officers. Arthrex argues that they are in fact principal officers because of the duties they execute and therefore must be appointed by the President.

Chief Justice Roberts wrote the majority opinion and ruled that the powers granted to the APJs via Congress are in violation of the Appointments Clause. The Court relied on its earlier decision in *Edmund v. United States*, which defined an inferior officer as someone who has "a superior other than the President."[11] This means an inferior officer must be directed and supervised at some level by leadership appointed by the President and confirmed by the Senate. The majority found that "Congress [had] assigned APJs 'significant authority' in adjudicating the public rights of private parties, while also insulating their decisions from review and their offices from removal" and is thus unconstitutional.[12]

The Court's solution was to give the Director authority over APJ actions to remedy the violation, as the Director is appointed by the President and consented to by the Senate. The Director now has the discretion to review APJ decisions, so that "the President remains responsible for the exercise of executive power—and through him, the exercise of executive power remains accountable to the people."[13] The majority reaffirmed *Edmond* with this ruling.

Justice Gorsuch concurred in part and dissented in part. He argued that patents should be considered a vested property right worthy of protection from the Executive Branch. He fears that the new statutory arrangement creates "a panel of bureaucrats [wielding] unreviewable power to take vested property rights."[14] Justice Gorsuch further explained his originalist perspective on the case, emphasizing his refusal to speculate on congressional intent despite any of the facts presented.

Justice Breyer, joined by Justices Sotomayor and Kagan, concurred in part and dissented in part. Justice Breyer wrote that Congress was well within its constitutional power to give agency leaders certain executive powers because the President can't do everything all of the time.

> *Given the technical nature of patents, the need for expertise, and the importance of avoiding political interference, Congress chose to grant the APJs a degree of independence. These considerations set forth a reasonable legislative objective sufficient to justify the restriction upon the Director's authority that Congress imposed.*[15]

Interestingly, Justice Thomas wrote the dissenting opinion, which was joined by Justices Breyer, Sotomayor and Kagan. It is not often to see this grouping of justices. Thomas strongly disagrees with the majority's approach and thinks the opinion evinces undue judicial activism. He argued that it should be for Congress to define the line between officer and inferior officer and that there was no Constitutional violation present. He wrote that prior decisions about the definition of inferior officers encompasses the APJ role. History does not support the majority's classification either, and in Justice Thomas's view, the Founding Fathers did not plan on such low level officials to be considered principal officers. He writes that "[t]he

Court today draws a new line dividing inferior officers from principal ones. The fact that this line places administrative patent judges on the side of Ambassadors, Supreme Court Justices, and department heads suggests that something is not quite right."[16]

Arthrex is important in offering some clarification of the line between officers and inferior officers. It makes clear that the Court will enforce this distinction and that it is quite formalistic in its approach. It opens the door to more challenges to countless administrative positions and will lead to much litigation, challenging power exercised by those not directly appointed by the President.

Removal Power

Twice in recent years, the Court has declared laws that limit presidential removal of executive branch officials unconstitutional. In *Free Enterprise Fund v. Public Company Accounting Oversight Board*,[17] the Court declared unconstitutional a provision of the Sarbanes-Oxley Act which created a Public Company Accounting Oversight Board (PCAOB) to oversee the accounting industry. The members of the Board are appointed by the Securities and Exchange Commission and are removable by the Commission only for "good cause." The issue was whether this is constitutional in light of the fact that the President cannot remove Board members and can remove members of the Securities and Exchange Commission also only for "good cause."

Chief Justice Roberts, writing for the Court in a 5–4 decision, declared the limit on removal unconstitutional. The Court declared:

> *We hold that such multilevel protection from removal is contrary to Article II's vesting of the executive power in the President. The President cannot "take Care that the Laws be faithfully executed" if he cannot oversee the faithfulness of the officers who execute them. Here, the President cannot remove an officer who enjoys more than one level of good-cause protection, even if the President determines that the officer is neglecting his duties or discharging them improperly. That judgment*

> *is instead committed to another officer, who may or may not agree with the President's determination, and whom the President cannot remove simply because that officer disagrees with him. This contravenes the President's "constitutional obligation to ensure the faithful execution of the laws."*[18]

A year ago, in *Seila Law LLC v. Consumer Financial Protection Bureau*, the Court held that having the Consumer Financial Protection Bureau led by a single director who cannot be removed by the President except for cause violated constitutional separation of powers.[19] Chief Justice Roberts wrote the opinion for the Court in the 5–4 decision and narrowly did so to focus just on the unconstitutionality of limiting presidential removal in an agency headed by a single director. But this is sure to lead to challenges against limits on presidential removal for other agencies as well.

The Court returned to the issue of limits on presidential removal this term in *Collins v. Yellen*.[20] The Federal National Mortgage Association (Fannie Mae, established in 1938) & Federal Home Loan Mortgage Corporation (Freddie Mac, established in 1970) are for profit corporations owned by private shareholders which operate under congressional charter. Their primary business is purchasing mortgages, pooling them into mortgage-backed securities, and selling them to investors. Both companies fell into a financial crisis with the rest of the country during the 2008 housing bubble, and Congress passed the Housing and Economic Recovery Act of 2008 in response. "Among other things, that law created the Federal Housing Finance Agency (FHFA), 'an independent agency' tasked with regulating the companies and, if necessary, stepping in as their conservator or receiver."[21] Fannie Mae and Freddie Mac were quickly put into conservatorship under FHFA.

The FHFA and the United States Treasury had made several agreements over the Recovery Act's lifetime, which were codified as four separate amendments to the act. After the third amendment instituted a new formula for calculating how much money the companies would pay to the Treasury, shareholders in both companies brought suit. The shareholders asked the Supreme Court to resolve two issues: (1) Whether the FHFA exceeded its statutory authority as the companies' conservator by adopting the third amendment; and (2) Whether the FHFA's leadership structure is unconstitutional because it is led by a single Director who may be removed by a President only "for cause."

Justice Alito, joined in full by Justices Roberts, Thomas, Kavanaugh, and Barrett wrote that the Court agreed with the second claim: FHFA's structure is unconstitutional and violates the separation of powers. Justice Thomas wrote a concurring opinion. Justices Gorsuch, Kagan and Sotomayor concurred in part. Justice Sotomayor also dissented in part and her opinion was joined by Justice Breyer.

Specifically, the Court found unconstitutional limiting the removal of the Director only "for cause by the President." The Court said that this encroaches on the President's power to remove officials and relied on the decision from the year before in *Seila Law LLC v. Consumer Financial Protection Bureau*. Justice Alito wrote "the Constitution prohibits even 'modest restrictions' on the President's power to remove the head of an agency with a single top officer."[22]

The statute was deemed unconstitutional, yet the shareholders were not granted the relief they requested. Justice Alito wrote that "[a]lthough the statute unconstitutionally limited the President's authority to remove the confirmed Directors, there was no constitutional defect in the statutorily prescribed method of appointment to that office."

Justices Kagan, Breyer and Sotomayor concurred only in judgement. Justice Kagan opined that the precedent case the majority relied on, *Selia Law*, was extended far beyond its intended reach. She writes that "[i]f an agency did not exercise 'significant executive power, the constitutionality of a removal restriction would remain an open question.'"[23] The holding here expands the President's power to remove executive officers even in situations that may not rise to the President's notice and consequently get in the way of the "real-world ability to carry out [their] agenda."[24]

Justice Sotomayor dissented and objected to the Court weakening the independence of agency leadership. She argued that the decision in *Seila Law* was inappropriately applied because it aimed to limit "single-director agency[s] with 'significant executive power.'"[25] Justice Sotomayor further objected that the Court's decision does not "afford Congress the freedom it has long possessed to make officers like the FHFA Director independent from Presidential control."[26]

Conclusion

Conservatives long have argued for a unitary executive where the President controls appointment and removal of federal officials. The decisions from this term follow the trend of recent cases in that regard.

It is important to note that the difference between the majority and the dissent is also a familiar pattern for separation of powers cases. The majority takes a formalistic approach to separation of powers and eschews any consideration of whether it would be desirable to create more independence of agencies. The dissent takes a functional approach about what is best from a policy perspective and seeks to protect the independence of agencies.

With a solid majority on the Court that would seek to limit Congress and protect presidential powers in appointments and removal, it is likely there will be many more challenges to federal laws and many more cases before the Supreme Court.

Endnotes

1. Lucia v S.E.C, 138 S. Ct. 2044 (2018).
2. Freytag. v. C.I.R., 501 U.S. 868, 881 (1991).
3. *Id.*
4. *Lucia*, *supra* note 1, at 2053.
5. *Id.* at 2057 (Breyer, J., concurring in the judgment in part and dissenting in part).
6. Carr v. Saul, 141 S. Ct. 1352 (2021).
7. *Id.* at 1361.
8. *Id.*
9. United States v. Arthrex, Inc. 141 U.S. 1970 (2021)
10. *Id.* at 1978.
11. Edmund v. United States, 520 U.S. 651, 662 (1997).
12. *Arthrex*, *supra* note 9, at 1986.
13. *Id.* at 1988.
14. *Id.* at 1989.
15. *Id.* at 1996 (Breyer, J., concurring in part and dissenting in part).
16. *Id.* at 1996 (Thomas, J., dissenting).
17. Free Enter. Fund v. Public Co. Acct. Oversight Bd., 561 U.S. 477 (2010).
18. *Id.* at 484.

19. Seila Law LLC v. Consumer Fin. Prot. Bureau, 140 S. Ct. 2183, 2204 (2020).
20. Collins v. Yellen, 141 U.S. 1761 (2021)
21. *Id.* at 1765.
22. *Id.* at 1787.
23. *Id.* at 1801 (Kagan, J., concurring in part and dissenting in part).
24. *Id.* at 1802.
25. *Id.* at 1805.
26. *Id.* at 1809 (Sotomayor, J., dissenting).

14

The Takings Clause

The Context: Types of Takings

The Fifth Amendment states "nor shall private property be taken for public use without just compensation." This provision, referred to as the "takings clause," was the focus of an important decision in October Term 2020, *Cedar Point Nursery v. Hassid*.[1] The Supreme Court has said that there are two kinds of takings: possessory and regulatory takings. In *Cedar Point Nursery*, the crucial issue was which kind of takings analysis was the appropriate one to use in reviewing California's law, a choice that likely would determine who would prevail in this dispute.

A "possessory taking" exists when the government confiscates or physically occupies property. The Supreme Court declared: "When faced with a constitutional challenge to a permanent physical occupation of real property, this Court has invariably found a taking."[2] For example, government confiscation of property pursuant to its eminent domain power always has been considered a classic taking. Also, the Court has repeatedly held that there is a taking when the government physically occupies property. Indeed, this type of taking is referred to as a "per se" taking. Quite importantly, a finding of a possessory taking does not mean that the government action is unconstitutional, but rather that the government must pay just compensation.

The other type of taking is called a "regulatory taking." In the landmark case *Pennsylvania Coal Co. v. Mahon*, in 1922, the Court said that a taking also could be found if government regulation of the use of property went "too far."[3] Since *Pennsylvania Coal Co.*, courts have struggled to decide what counts as too far. The Supreme Court developed a balancing test for deciding whether there is a regulatory taking. In *Penn Central Transportation Co. v. New York City*, the Court first articulated general criteria that should be considered in evaluating whether a regulation is a taking.[4] In a later case, the Court elaborated:

> *[W]e have eschewed the development of any set formula for identifying a "taking" forbidden by the Fifth Amendment, and have relied instead on ad hoc, factual inquiries into the circumstances of each particular case. To aid in this determination, however, we have identified three factors which have "particular significance": (1) the economic impact of the regulation on the claimant; (2) the extent to which the regulation has interfered with investment-backed expectations; and (3) the character of the governmental action.*[5]

These criteria accord courts a tremendous amount of discretion, so it is not surprising that cases concerning regulatory takings are often inconsistent and difficult to reconcile with each other. As the criteria indicate, the Court especially focuses on the economic effect of the government regulations and the extent to which they interfere with reasonable expectations of the property owner.

One important principle that emerges from the cases, and that is crucial in judicial consideration of regulatory takings, is that government regulation is a taking if it leaves no reasonable economically viable use of property. Government regulation is not a taking simply because it decreases the value of a person's property, so long as it leaves reasonable economically viable uses.

The determination of the type of taking often has important consequences on the outcome of a case. Possessory takings analysis is more favorable to challengers of government actions, while regulatory takings analysis is more favorable for the government. That is why parties challenging a government action as a taking want the court to characterize it as a possessory taking: doing so means the action will be deemed a taking. But those defending the government action will encourage the court to look at whether it constitutes a regulatory taking. The crucial issue in *Cedar Point Nursery v. Hassid* is whether a California law should be seen as a possessory or a regulatory taking.

The Court's Decision in *Cedar Point Nursery v. Hassid*

California law requires that agricultural employers must allow union organizers onto their property for up to three hours per day, 120 days per year to speak to employees. The California Agricultural Labor Relations Board promulgated a regulation over the self-organization rights of employees that includes "the right of access by union organizers to the premises of an agricultural employer for the purpose of meeting and talking with employees and soliciting their support."[6] Under the regulation, labor organizations may "take access" to an agricultural employer's property for up to four 30-day periods in one calendar year.[7] The rule allows two organizers per work crew (plus one additional organizer for every 15 workers over 30 workers in a crew) to enter the employer's property for up to one hour before work, one hour during the lunch break, and one hour after work. Organizers may meet and talk with employees, but cannot engage in disruptive behavior. Employers who interfere with this right of access can be charged with an unfair labor practice, which can result in sanctions against the employer.

Two farms—Cedar Point Nursery (a strawberry grower) and Fowler Packing Company (a grower and shipper of table grapes and citrus)—brought a challenge to this law and regulation contending that it constituted a possessory taking.

The Supreme Court, in a 6–3 decision, agreed with the farms, holding that the California law constitutes a possessory taking. Chief Justice Roberts wrote the opinion for the Court, joined by Justices Thomas, Alito, Gorsuch, Kavanaugh, and Barrett. Justice Breyer wrote a dissenting opinion, joined by Justices Sotomayor and Kagan. The Court concluded:

> *The access regulation appropriates a right to invade the growers' property and therefore constitutes a per se physical taking. The regulation grants union organizers a right to physically enter and occupy the growers' land for three hours per day, 120 days per year. Rather than restraining the growers' use of their own property, the regulation appropriates for the enjoyment of third parties the owners' right to exclude.*[8]

The Court explained that a core component of property rights is the power to exclude. Chief Justice Roberts said that the California law and regulation, by their very terms, takes this right away from property owners by giving union organizers a right to be present on their property. The fact that organizers were present only for some days and some hours did not matter to the Court. For the majority, "a physical appropriation is a taking whether it is permanent or temporary."[9]

There are myriad regulations that require that government inspectors have access to private property. How is this labor regulation different from those regulations? Chief Justice Roberts wrote:

> *[T]he government may require property owners to cede a right of access as a condition of receiving certain benefits, without causing a taking . . . Under this framework, government health and safety inspection regimes will generally not constitute takings. When the government conditions the grant of a benefit such as a permit, license, or registration on allowing access for reasonable health and safety inspections, both the nexus and rough proportionality requirements of the constitutional conditions framework should not be difficult to satisfy.*[10]

The Court concluded that the California law, by granting a right of access to property, constituted a *per se* possessory taking. The Court did not reach the question of appropriate remedy since that question was not before it.

Justice Breyer wrote a forceful dissent. Breyer disagreed that the California law should be regarded as a physical appropriation of the owners' property. He wrote:

> *[T]his regulation does not "appropriate" anything; it regulates the employers' right to exclude others. At the same time, our prior cases make clear that the regulation before us allows only a temporary invasion of a landowner's property and that this kind of temporary invasion amounts to a taking only if it goes "too far." In my view, the majority's conclusion threatens to make many ordinary forms of regulation unusually complex or impractical.*[11]

Justice Breyer stressed that the government was not appropriating private property for its own use and that it was not a permanent physical occupation of property. He saw the law as a regulation. This meant it should have been analyzed as to whether it is a regulatory taking, not a possessory taking. He wrote:

> *The regulation does not appropriate anything. It does not take from the owners a right to invade (whatever that might mean). It does not give the union organizations the right to exclude anyone. It does not give the government the right to exclude anyone. What does it do? It gives union organizers the right temporarily to invade a portion of the property owners' land. It thereby limits the landowners' right to exclude certain others. The regulation regulates (but does not appropriate) the owners' right to exclude.*[12]

Implications

The decision illustrates the great importance of the distinction between possessory and regulatory takings. If a court deems a government action to be the former, then it is a *per se* taking requiring just compensation. But if it is the latter, then the action is analyzed under the *Penn Central* test as to whether the government went too far, and the government has a much greater chance of prevailing.

The Court's decision raises important questions. First, there is a tension between this decision and other instances where the government granted access rights, but its action was treated as a regulatory taking. For example, the Court consistently has said that conditions on development that create a right of access to property are analyzed as regulatory takings. In *Nollan v. California Coastal Commission*, the government conditioned a permit for development of beachfront property on the owner granting the public an easement to cross the property for beach access.[13] The Court, in an opinion by Justice Scalia, said that there would be a taking if the government were to require the property owners to grant a permanent easement. He wrote:

> *Had California simply required the [appellants] to make an easement across their beachfront property available to the public on a permanent basis . . . we have no doubt there would have been a taking . . . We think a "permanent physical occupation" has occurred . . . where individuals are given a permanent and continuous right to pass to and fro, so that the real property may continuously be traversed, even though no particular individual is permitted to station himself permanently upon the premises.*[14]

But the Court said that because it was not a "permanent physical occupation" it was not a taking. The California law and regulation in *Cedar Point* was also not a permanent physical occupation, yet the Court came to exactly the opposite conclusion.

The Court in *Nollan* said that the condition had to be analyzed as to whether it was a regulatory taking and held that police power allows the government to place a condition on development if it is rationally related to preventing harms caused by the new construction. The Court said that conditions on development are not a regulatory taking so long as the benefit to the government is roughly proportionate to the burden imposed. The Court reaffirmed this holding in a subsequent case, *Dolan v. City of Tigard*.[15]

But why are these considered mere regulatory takings, while the California law in *Cedar Point* is a possessory taking? What if California conditioned the development of agriculture property on allowing union access? Would that transform the analysis into a review of regulatory taking?

Another example of the Court previously applying a regulatory taking analysis for government-granted access rights was in *PruneYard Shopping Center v. Robins*, where the Court rejected the claim that there was a taking when the California Supreme Court interpreted the California Constitution as requiring that shopping centers be open to speech activities.[16] After an earlier ruling to the contrary, the Supreme Court in *Hudgens v. NLRB* held that there was not a First Amendment right of access to privately owned shopping centers for speech purposes.[17] However, in *PruneYard*, the California Supreme Court found that there was a *state* constitutional right to use shopping centers for speech activities.[18] The owners appealed this ruling to the Supreme Court, arguing that mandating access to the shopping center was a taking because it would result in a physical invasion of the property.

The Supreme Court, in an opinion by Justice Rehnquist, concluded that there was no taking. The Court said that

> *[t]here is nothing to suggest that preventing appellants from prohibiting this sort of activity will unreasonably impair the value or use of their property as a shopping center . . . In these circumstances, the fact that they may have 'physically invaded' appellants' property cannot be viewed as determinative.*[19]

But under the particular analysis used by the Court in *Cedar Point*, why wouldn't mandatory access to shopping centers be deemed a possessory taking? After all, *PruneYard* was a case where California law was granting a right of access to private property, just like the challenged regulation in *Cedar Point*. Chief Justice Roberts addressed the discrepancy, writing: "Unlike the growers' properties, the PruneYard was open to the public, welcoming some 25,000 patrons a day. Limitations on how a business generally open to the public may treat individuals on the premises are readily distinguishable from regulations granting a right to invade property closed to the public."[20] Roberts's reasoning begs the question of why a property owner who chooses to give access to some cannot exercise control, as a property owner, to exclude others. Put another way, why was the government-granted right of access in *PruneYard* analyzed as a regulatory taking, but in *Cedar Point* it was considered as a possessory taking? It is unclear why opening the property to the public for other purposes—shopping, but not labor union activity—changes the framework for takings analysis.[21]

Second, how is this to be distinguished from all of the instances where the government requires that property owners grant access for inspections? The fact that such actions are temporary does not matter under the Court's analysis in *Cedar Point*. The Court addressed this concern and said:

> *[T]he government may require property owners to cede a right of access as a condition of receiving certain benefits, without causing a taking . . . Under this framework, government health and safety inspection regimes will generally not constitute takings. When the government conditions the grant of a benefit such as a permit, license, or registration on allowing access for reasonable health and safety inspections, both the nexus and rough proportionality requirements of the constitutional conditions framework should not be difficult to satisfy.*[22]

But if the government can condition ownership of property on allowing inspectors access because of the public benefit, why isn't the benefit of labor organizing and labor peace also sufficient? If the government can require that agricultural growers allow health inspectors access without it being a possessory taking, why can't they do the same for union organizers? The *Cedar Point* majority fails to answer that question.

Finally, what is the remedy for this class of taking? The takings clause does not prohibit government action, but rather it requires that the government pay just compensation for the taking. But what would that look like in *Cedar Point*? What, if anything, is the loss to the owner, in reasonable market value terms, of allowing union access to the property? Unless this is measured in terms of additional costs to be incurred if workers unionize, it is hard to find any loss to the owner.

Conclusion

All would agree, I am sure, that the Roberts Court overall is pro-business, pro-property rights, and consistently rules against labor unions. All three prongs converged in *Cedar Point* to produce the reasoning for the case. But the Court's approach, treating a law granting a right of access as a *per se* taking, is sure to lead to a great deal of litigation challenging other government laws that provide access to private property.

Endnotes

1. 141 S. Ct. 2063 (2021).
2. Loretto v. Teleprompter Manhattan CATV Corp., 458 U.S. 419, 427 (1982).
3. 260 U.S. 393, 415 (1922).
4. 438 U.S. 104 (1978).
5. Connolly v. Pension Benefit Guar. Corp., 475 U.S. 211, 224-25 (1986) (citations omitted).
6. 141 S. Ct. at 2069 (citing Cal. Code Regs., tit. 8, § 20900(e)).
7. *Id.*
8. *Id.* at 2072.
9. *Id.* at 2074.
10. *Id.* at 2079 (citations omitted).
11. *Id.* at 2081 (Breyer, J., dissenting).
12. *Id.* at 2083 (Breyer, J., dissenting).
13. 483 U.S. 825 (1987).
14. *Id.* at 831–32.
15. 512 U.S. 374 (1994).
16. 447 U.S. 74 (1980).
17. 424 U.S. 507 (1976).
18. 23 Cal. 3d 899, 592 P.2d 341 (1979).
19. 447 U.S. at 83–84.
20. Cedar Point Nursery v. Hassid, 141 S. Ct. 2063, 2076–77 (2021).
21. 447 U.S. at 83.
22. 141 S. Ct. at 2079 (citations omitted).

15

Voting Rights

The Context

The United States has a long and disgraceful history of race discrimination with regard to voting. The Fourteenth Amendment, ratified in 1868, provides that no state may deny any person equal protection of the laws. Two years later, the Fifteenth Amendment was ratified to explicitly deal with the problem of race discrimination in voting. It states: "The right of citizens of the United States to vote shall not be denied or abridged by the United States or by any State on account of race, color, or previous condition of servitude."

As a result of these amendments, and Reconstruction, more than a half million African American men in the South became voters in the 1870s. There was a dramatic effect to this enfranchisement of Black men. In Mississippi, for example, former slaves were half of the state's population and Mississippi elected two black United States Senators and a number of Black state officials, including a lieutenant governor.

Because of the compromise that decided the 1876 election, Reconstruction was ended, and Northern troops were withdrawn from the South. Southern states quickly adopted laws to deny rights to former slaves and to segregate every aspect of life. Southern states also adopted multiple laws designed to keep Blacks from voting. Poll taxes were implemented, requiring that individuals pay a fee to vote. Literacy tests were adopted, requiring a person to read a section of the state constitution to a county clerk and then explain it before registering to vote. The clerk, who was always white, had discretion to decide whether the person was sufficiently literate. Southern states also enacted a "grandfather clause" that created an exception to the literacy tests for those whose grandfathers were qualified to vote before the Civil War. Obviously, this benefited only white citizens.

These discriminatory actions worked as intended. For example, in Mississippi, the percentage of Black voting-age men registered to vote fell from over 90 percent during Reconstruction to less than 6 percent in 1892. Beyond the laws that kept African-Americans from voting, intimidation tactics were directed at those who tried to register and vote. As a result, just three percent of voting-age Black men and women in the South were registered to vote in 1940. In Mississippi, under one percent were registered.[1]

The civil rights movement worked to combat race discrimination in voting and to increase Black voter registration. Still, "[b]y 1965, only 27% of black Georgians, 19% of black Alabamians, and 7%—yes, 7%—of black Mississippians were registered to vote."[2]

Voting Rights Act of 1965

A fundamental change occurred when Congress passed the Voting Rights Act of 1965, one of the most important civil rights statutes adopted in American history. There were two key provisions of the Voting Rights Act. Section 2 of the Act prohibits voting practices or procedures that discriminate on the basis of race or against certain language minority groups. It further provided that lawsuits can be brought to challenge state or local actions that are alleged to violate Section 2.

In 1980, in *City of Mobile v. Bolden*, the Supreme Court held that proving race discrimination in voting—whether under the Fourteenth Amendment's equal protection clause or the Fifteenth Amendment or Section 2 of the Voting Rights Act—requires proof of a discriminatory intent.[3] In 1982, Congress amended the Voting Rights Act to provide that discriminatory impact would be sufficient to show a violation of the law. Section 2 was revised to provide that a plaintiff could establish a violation of the section if the evidence established that, in the context of the "totality of the circumstance of the local electoral process," the standard, practice, or procedure being challenged had the result of denying a racial or language minority an equal opportunity to participate in the political process.

Another crucial provision of the Voting Rights Act, Section 5, was effectively nullified by the Supreme Court in *Shelby County v. Holder* in 2013.[4] Congress, when adopting the Voting Rights Act, realized that allowing lawsuits to challenge election procedures was not adequate to stop discrimination in voting. Election litigation is expensive and time consuming. Congress was aware that Southern states often invented new ways of disenfranchising minority voters. The arcade game "whack-a-mole" seems an apt analogy to the states' seemingly endless discriminatory inventions. A state would adopt a law to limit voting by racial minorities. Then, the law would be challenged and struck down or withdrawn, only to be replaced by a new voting restriction. Section 5 of the Voting Rights Act was adopted to prevent such actions.

Section 5 applies to jurisdictions with a history of race discrimination in voting and requires that there be preapproval—termed "preclearance"—of any attempt to change "any voting qualification or prerequisite to voting, or standard, practice, or procedure with respect to voting" in any covered jurisdiction.[5] The preapproval must come either from the Attorney General of the United States, through an administrative procedure in the Department of Justice, or from a three-judge federal court in the District of Columbia through a request for a declaratory judgment. Section 4(B) delineated the formula to be used to determine which jurisdictions needed to get preclearance.

In 2006, after extensive hearings, Congress voted overwhelmingly—98-0 in the Senate and 390-33 in the House—to extend Section 5 for 25 years. It did not change Section 4(B) or Section 5. Congress expressly concluded that voting discrimination persists in the covered jurisdictions and that without Section 5, "minority citizens will be deprived of the opportunity to exercise their right to vote, or will have their votes diluted, undermining the significant gains made by minorities in the last 40 years."[6]

The record before Congress supported this conclusion. For example, between 1982-2006, the Section 5 preclearance requirement blocked over 700 discriminatory changes in election systems in covered jurisdictions.[7] Another 205 discriminatory changes were withdrawn. Countless potential changes were not adopted because of the recognition that preclearance was unlikely. The continued discrimination in covered jurisdictions is further evidenced by 650 successful court challenges under Section 2 of the Voting Rights Act in these places. University of Michigan Law Professor Ellen Katz undertook extensive studies which found that covered jurisdictions have only 25% of the country's population, but account for 56% of the successful suits under Section 2.[8]

Despite this, in *Shelby County, Alabama v. Holder*, for the first time since the Nineteenth century, the Supreme Court struck down a federal civil rights statute. In a 5–4 decision, the Court declared unconstitutional Section 4(B) of the Voting Rights Act.[9] As explained above, this is the provision which determines which jurisdictions must get preclearance. Without Section 4(B), Section 5 is meaningless; no jurisdictions need to get preclearance. Chief Justice Roberts, writing for the Court, stressed that the formula in Section 4(B), last modified in 1982, rests on data from the 1960s and the 1970s and that race discrimination in voting has changed since then. The Court declared:

> *Nearly 50 years later, things have changed dramatically. Shelby County contends that the preclearance requirement, even without regard to its disparate coverage, is now unconstitutional. Its arguments have a good deal of force. In the covered jurisdictions, [v]oter turnout and registration rates now approach parity. Blatantly discriminatory evasions of federal decrees are rare. And minority candidates hold office at unprecedented levels. The tests and devices that blocked access to the ballot have been forbidden nationwide for over 40 years.*[10]

Thus, "[c]overage today is based on decades-old data and eradicated practices."[11]

The Court pointed to the intrusion on the covered states, noting they could not exercise the power to choose how to hold elections, but instead the "States must beseech the Federal Government for permission to implement laws that they would otherwise have the right to enact and execute on their own, subject of course to any injunction in a § 2 action."[12] The Court also emphasized that Sections 4(B) and 5, by requiring only some states to get preclearance, violated the principle of equal state sovereignty. The Court stated: "Not only do States retain sovereignty under the Constitution, there is also a 'fundamental principle of *equal* sovereignty' among the States . . . [D]espite the tradition of equal sovereignty, the Act applies to only nine States (and several additional counties)."[13] But the Court in *Shelby County* stressed that Section 2 still was available to challenge discriminatory election systems.

There is no doubt that the invalidation of preclearance has had an effect. In the most recent case, *Brnovich v. Democratic National Committee*, Justice Kagan noted, "Although causation is hard to establish definitively, those post *Shelby County* changes appear to have reduced minority participation in the next election cycle. The most comprehensive study available found that in areas freed from Section 5 review, white turnout remained the same, but 'minority participation dropped by 2.1 percentage points'—a stark reversal in direction from prior elections. The results, said the scholar who crunched the numbers, 'provide early evidence that the Shelby ruling may jeopardize decades of voting rights progress.'"[14]

Brnovich v. Democratic National Committee

The cases before the Court this term challenged two provisions of Arizona law. One says that a ballot is not to be counted if it was cast by a person outside of his or her precinct. The other prohibits "ballot harvesting," making it a felony to collect and deliver another person's completed ballot (with exceptions for family members, caregivers, mail carriers and election officials).

Lawsuits were brought by the Democratic National Committee and voters challenging these provisions. They argued that these Arizona laws violate Section 2 of the Voting Rights Act because they have a discriminatory effect against minority voters. The plaintiffs also alleged a discriminatory intent behind the laws and claimed that they violate the Constitution as well as the Voting Rights Act.

The United States District Court, after a 10-day trial, ruled for the defendants, and the United States Court of Appeals for the Ninth Circuit, in a 2–1 decision, affirmed. But the Ninth Circuit granted *en banc* review and reversed, ruling for the plaintiffs in a 7–4 decision. Judge William Fletcher wrote the opinion for the Court. The Court said

> *[w]e hold that Arizona's policy of wholly discarding, rather than counting or partially counting, out-of-precinct ballots, and H.B. 2023's criminalization of the collection of another person's ballot, have a discriminatory impact on American Indian, Hispanic, and African American voters in Arizona, in violation of the "results test" of Section 2 of the VRA. We hold, further, that H.B. 2023's criminalization of the collection of another person's ballot was enacted with discriminatory intent, in violation of the 'intent test' of Section 2 of the VRA and of the Fifteenth Amendment.*[15]

The Ninth Circuit found that both the prohibition on out-of-precinct voting and on ballot harvesting violated this test. For example, the Court noted that during the three general elections leading up to the 2020 election, Native Americans, Hispanics and African Americans in Arizona were twice as likely as whites to vote outside of the precinct to which they had been assigned and therefore to have their votes not counted. The court likewise said that the prohibition on ballot harvesting had a discriminatory effect against minority voters, and moreover that it was motivated by a discriminatory intent.

The Supreme Court granted review. One interesting aspect of the case before the Court involves the shift from the Trump to the Biden administration. The Trump administration filed a brief on behalf of Arizona to reverse the Ninth Circuit. On Tuesday, February 16, 2021, the Solicitor General's office informed the Supreme Court that the new administration reconsidered the issues in the case and that it "does not disagree" with the previous administration's stance on the Arizona laws. However, the memo also stated that the Department of Justice "does not adhere to the framework for application of Section 2 in vote-denial cases" laid out in the Trump administration's brief.

The Supreme Court, in a 6–3 decision reversed the Ninth Circuit and ruled in favor of Arizona. Justice Alito wrote the opinion for the Court, joined by Chief Justice Roberts and Justices Thomas, Gorsuch, Kavanaugh, and Barrett. Justice Kagan wrote the dissent, joined by Justices Sotomayor and Breyer.

Justice Alito began by noting that prior Supreme Court cases about Section 2 of the Voting Rights Act arose in the context of vote dilution claims, specifically as to whether drawing of election districts discriminated against minority voters. Justice Alito noted that this was the first time the Court had considered the application of Section 2 to the voting restrictions focusing on the time, place, or manner of voting. He said that under Section 2 the focus must be on the totality of the circumstances.

In a crucial part of the opinion, Justice Alito said that the model for identifying racial discrimination based on disparate impact that is used to interpret many other federal civil rights laws was "not useful" here."[16] He wrote that defining discrimination based on disparate impact "would have the effect of invalidating a great many neutral voting regulations with long pedigrees that are reasonable means of pursuing legitimate interests."[17]

Justice Alito went on to list five factors that courts must consider when a voting rule is challenged under Section 2:

- *The size of the burden imposed on voters.* Justice Alito wrote:

  After all, every voting rule imposes a burden of some sort. Voting takes time and, for almost everyone, some travel, even if only to a nearby mailbox. Casting a vote, whether by following the directions for using a voting machine or completing a paper ballot, requires compliance with certain rules. But because voting necessarily requires some effort and compliance with some rules, the concept of a voting system that is "equally open' and that furnishes an equal 'opportunity' to cast a ballot must tolerate the "usual burdens of voting."[18]

- *The degree to which the rule deviates from the rule in effect in 1982, when Section 2 was last amended.* The Court said that the "degree to which a voting rule departs from what was standard practice when § 2 was amended in 1982 is a relevant consideration. Because every voting rule imposes a burden of some sort, it is useful to have benchmarks with which the burdens imposed by a challenged rule can be compared."[19] The Court chose 1982 because that is the year that the Voting Rights Act was amended by Congress.

- *The scale of any disparate racial impact.* The Court said,

  The size of any disparities in a rule's impact on members of different racial or ethnic groups is also an important factor to consider. Small disparities are less likely than large ones to indicate that a system is not equally open. To the extent that minority and non-minority groups differ with respect to employment, wealth, and education, even neutral regulations, no matter how crafted, may well result in some predictable disparities in rates of voting and noncompliance with voting rules. But the mere fact there is some disparity in impact does not necessarily mean that a system is not equally open or that it does not give everyone an equal opportunity to vote. The size of any disparity matters. And in assessing the size of any disparity, a meaningful comparison is essential. What are at bottom very small differences should not be artificially magnified.[20]

- *The opportunities to vote provided by the state's overall system.* The Court said: "[W]here a State provides multiple ways to vote, any burden imposed on voters who choose one of the available options cannot be evaluated without also taking into account the other available means."[21]

- *The strength of the state interests served by the rule—such as preventing fraud.* The Court said that

  every voting rule imposes a burden of some sort, and therefore, in determining 'based on the totality of circumstances' whether a rule goes too far, it is important to consider the reason for the

> *rule. Rules that are supported by strong state interests are less likely to violate § 2. One strong and entirely legitimate state interest is the prevention of fraud.*[22]

The Court applied these five factors and concluded that the Arizona law did not violate Section 2 of the Voting Rights Act. The Court found a relatively minor burden on voting and on voters of color, while seeing the Arizona requirements as furthering important government interests. The Court also reversed the Ninth Circuit's conclusion that there was a racially discriminatory intent, concluding that the district court's finding of no discrimination was not "clear error."

Justice Kagan wrote a vehement dissent. She said that the factors identified by the Court had no basis in the statute. She said:

> *Wherever it can, the majority gives a cramped reading to broad language. And then it uses that reading to uphold two election laws from Arizona that discriminate against minority voters. . . . This is not how the Court is supposed to interpret and apply statutes. But that ordinary critique woefully undersells the problem. What is tragic here is that the Court has (yet again) rewritten—in order to weaken—a statute that stands as a monument to America's greatness, and protects against its basest impulses. What is tragic is that the Court has damaged a statute designed to bring about the end of discrimination in voting.*[23]

Justice Kagan argued that the statistics demonstrated that the Arizona election restrictions had a significant discriminatory effect against minority voters and should be deemed to violate Section 2 of the Voting Rights Act. The dissent stressed that the five factors identified in the majority opinion have no basis in the statute and abandon the usual approach to finding disparate impact under federal civil right laws.

Implications

There is no doubt that the Court's decision will make it much harder to use Section 2 of the Voting Rights Act to challenge state laws imposing restrictions on voting. The five factors articulated by Justice Alito all point in one direction: making it more difficult to find a violation of Section 2 of the Voting Rights Act. This is particularly important now because many states have adopted new laws that restrict voting and that likely will be shown to have a discriminatory impact against minority voters. As Justice Kagan noted:

> *In recent months, State after State has taken up or enacted legislation erecting new barriers to voting. Those laws shorten the time polls are open, both on Election Day and before. They impose new prerequisites to voting by mail, and shorten the windows to apply for and return mail ballots. They make it harder to register to vote, and easier to purge voters from the rolls. Two laws even ban handing out food or water to voters standing in line.*[24]

The laws all have been adopted in states with Republican legislatures and all are designed to make voting more difficult for counties, districts, and precincts that voted more Democratic. Because Black Americans vote for Democratic candidates about 90% of the time, many of these restrictions undoubtedly will have a discriminatory impact. The Court's decision in *Brnovich* will make successful challenges far more difficult.

There are two widely different perspectives on voting in the United States. Republicans see voter fraud as a major problem and favor laws like Arizona's that limit voting. Democrats see voter suppression, especially of minority voters, as a major problem and see Arizona's law as accomplishing exactly that and say that significant voter fraud is unproven. The Court has six justices appointed by Republican Presidents and three by Democratic Presidents. The majority has clearly adopted the Republican viewpoint about voting.

The Court's decision will have a profound effect on what state laws are enacted and allowed regarding voting, and on who votes and how elections are conducted for many years to come.

Endnotes

1. Steven F. Lawson, Running for Freedom: Civil Rights and Black Politics in America Since 1941 21, 28 (Wiley 2014).

2. Brnovich v. Democratic Nat'l Comm., 141 S. Ct. 2321, 2353 (2021) (Kagan, J., dissenting).

3. Mobile v. Bolden, 446 U.S. 55, 79–80 (1980).

4. Shelby Cty. v. Holder, 570 U.S. 529 (2013).

5. Voting Rights Act of 1965, 89 Pub. L. No. 89-110, § 5, 79 Stat. 437, 439.

6. Fannie Lou Hamer, Rosa Parks, and Coretta Scott King Voting Rights Act Reauthorization and Amendments Act of 2006, 109 P.L. 246, § 2(b)(9), 120 Stat. 577, 578.

7. *Shelby Cty., supra* note 4, at 571 (Ginsburg, J., dissenting) (citing to H.R. Rep. No. 109-478, at 21).

8. *Id.* at 577.

9. *Id.* at 566–567.

10. *Id.* at 547 (citations omitted).

11. *Id.* at 551.

12. *Id.* at 544.

13. *Id.*

14. *Brnovich, supra* note 2, at 2353 (Kagan, J., dissenting).

15. Democratic Nat'l Comm. v. Hobbs, 948 F.3d 989, 999 (9th Cir. 2020).

16. *Brnovich, supra* note 2, at 2340 ("We also do not find the disparate-impact model employed in Title VII and Fair Housing Act cases useful here.").

17. *Id.* at 2341.

18. *Id.* at 2338.

19. *Id.*

20. *Id.* at 2339.

21. *Id.*

22. *Id.* at 2339–40.

23. *Id.* at 2351 (Kagan, J. dissenting).

24. *Id.* at 2356.

16

Conclusions: Looking Ahead

It often has been remarked that every time there is a new justice, it is a different Court. There have been three new justices, a third of the Court, who have been appointed in the last four years: Neil Gorsuch, Brett Kavanaugh, and Amy Coney Barrett. All are relatively young—in their late 40s or early 50s when they became justices—and all were selected by President Donald Trump because of their staunch conservativism.

They join a Court that already had two of the most conservative justices in American history in Clarence Thomas and Samuel Alito. The crucial question is what will it mean to have a Court with such a solid conservative majority. Of course, this is something political conservatives applaud and political liberals lament, but no one denies the existence of a solid conservative majority on the high Court.

October Term 2020 provided a glimpse of this. There was no closely divided case where the liberal justices were in the majority. The Court moved the law in a direction favored by conservatives in a number of important areas: free exercise of religion, freedom of association, standing, separation of powers, the Takings Clause, separation of powers, and voting rights.

One striking, but less obvious aspect of the Court's conservatism was its lack of deference to the other branches and levels of government. Over 30 years ago, I described the central tenet of the conservatism of the Rehnquist Court as being about deference, especially to the decisions of elected officials.[1] But that is not the conservatism of the Roberts Court. Its most important decisions this term—in areas such as religion, speech, separation of powers, takings, and voting—without exception ruled against the government. No longer is "judicial restraint" a core aspect of conservative constitutional jurisprudence.

As I said in the Introduction, it is important to be cautious about generalizing too much from one term of the Court. There were only 54 decisions. Justice Barrett did not participate in the October oral arguments or decisions of those cases. She therefore was part of only about 44 cases, hardly enough for any definitive assessments.

But the coming term, October Term 2021 likely will tell us much more about the newly constituted Roberts Court. Most notably, in *Dobbs v. Jackson Women's Health Organization*, the Court has granted review on the issue of "[w]hether all pre-viability prohibitions on elective abortions are unconstitutional."[2] In *Roe v. Wade*, in 1973, the Court held that the government cannot prohibit abortions prior to viability.[3] In *Planned Parenthood v. Casey*, in 1992, the Court said that it was reaffirming the "essential holding" of *Roe* that states could not prohibit abortions before viability.[4]

Viability is generally thought to be the twenty-third or twenty-fourth week of pregnancy; no one puts it earlier than the twenty-second week. The Mississippi law before the Court in *Dobbs* prohibits abortions after the fifteenth week of pregnancy. Other states—such as Texas, Iowa, and Ohio—prohibit abortions once a fetal heartbeat can be detected, about the sixth week of pregnancy. The issue in *Dobbs* is whether the Supreme Court will explicitly or effectively overrule *Roe v. Wade*.

The Court also has on its docket for October Term 2021 *New York State Rifle & Pistol Association v. Corlett*, which challenges the New York law restricting carrying concealed weapons.[5] New York requires a permit for having a concealed weapon and is very restrictive as to being able to obtain them. In *District of Columbia v. Heller*, in 2008, the Supreme Court for the first time in American history declared unconstitutional a law as violating the Second Amendment.[6] The Court held that the Second

Amendment protects a right to have guns in the home for the sake of security. The Court has denied certiorari in over 100 Second Amendment cases since 2008, but now has before it a case that will give it the opportunity to decide whether there is a constitutional right to have guns outside the home and to have concealed weapons.

And there is a petition for certiorari pending in *Students for Fair Admissions v. Harvard*, which concerns whether Harvard University's affirmative action program violated Title VI of the 1964 Civil Rights Act, which prohibits recipients of federal funds from discriminating based on race.[7] The Court's composition has changed dramatically since the Court last upheld affirmative action in 2016 in *Fisher v. University of Texas*, with both Justices Kennedy and Ginsburg being part of a narrow majority.[8]

There are no more controversial legal issues in the United States than abortion, gun rights, and affirmative action. There are no legal issues where the divide between liberals and conservatives is more evident. All might be before the Court in October Term 2021.

In 1968, Richard Nixon ran for President by sharply attacking the liberal Warren Court and promising to appoint "strict constructionists." The Reagan presidency renewed this quest for a conservative Court and pursued it openly and aggressively. Now after a half century, their goal of a very conservative majority on the Supreme Court has been achieved. October Term 2020 provides a glimpse of what it will mean, but next year will give us even more of an indication.

Endnotes

1. Erwin Chemerinsky, *Foreword: The Vanishing Constitution*, 103 HARV. L. REV. 43 (1989).
2. 945 F.3d 265 (5th Cir. 2020), *cert. granted*, 141 S. Ct. ___ (2021).
3. 410 U.S. 113 (1973).
4. 505 U.S. 833, 835 (1992).
5. 818 Fed.Appx. 99 (2d Cir. 2020), *cert. granted*, 141 S. Ct. ___ (2021).
6. 554 U.S. 570 (2008).
7. 980 F.3d 157 (1st Cir. 2020).
8. 136 S. Ct. 2198 (2016).

Index